Floors & Floor Coverings

Created by the Editorial Staff of Ortho Books

Project Editor
Jill Fox

Writers and Consultants
B. Gay Ballard
Robert J. Beckstrom
Daniel Fuller
Harriett L. Kirk
Diane Dorrans Saeks

Illustrator
Edith Allgood

Principle Photographer
Kenneth Rice

Ortho Books

Publisher
Edward A. Evans

Editorial Director
Christine Jordan

Production Director
Ernie S. Tasaki

Managing Editors
Robert J. Beckstrom
Michael D. Smith
Sally W. Smith

System Manager
Linda M. Bouchard

Product Manager
Richard E. Pile, Jr.

Distribution Specialist
Barbara F. Steadham

Operations Assistant
Georgiann Wright

Administrative Assistant
Francine Lorentz-Olson

Technical Consultant
J. A. Crozier, Jr., Ph.D.

Address all inquiries to:
Ortho Books
Chevron Chemical Company
Consumer Products Division
Box 5047
San Ramon, CA 94583

ISBN 0-89721-228-2
Library of Congress Catalog Card Number 90-84631

Chevron Chemical Company
6001 Bollinger Canyon Road, San Ramon, CA 94583

Acknowledgments

Additional Consultants
Walter D. Anderson
  Resilient Floor Covering
  Institute
Pete Hambleton
  Kentile Floors, Inc.
John Hanson
  American Biltrite
George D. Pillow, Jr.
  National Floor Products, Inc.
H. G. Stoudt
  Tarkett, Inc.
Walter Whitley
  National Oak Flooring
  Manufacturers' Association,
  Inc.

Copy Chief
Melinda E. Levine

Editorial Coordinator
Cass Dempsey

Copyeditor
Irene Elmer

Proofreader
Nancy Beckus

Indexer
Elinor Lindheimer

Editorial Assistant
John Parr

Composition by
Laurie A. Steele

Production by
Lezlly Freier

Separations by
Color Tech. Corp.

Lithographed in the USA by
Webcrafters, Inc.

Special Thanks
Susan Anderson
  Armstrong World
  Industries, Inc.
Lesley D. Axelrod
  Creamer Dickson Basford
Mannington Resilient Floors
Benefit Guild of the East Bay
  1990 Designer Showcase
Designer's Showcase Home
  1990 Sponsored by the
  American Cancer Society and
  the Peninsula Chapter of
  A.S.I.D.
The San Francisco Decorator
  Showcase 1990

Homeowners
Pam Anderson and
  Robert Blackstone
Allan and Syde Bortez
Cynthia Brian
Betsie Corwin
Dr. Victoria Flavell
Susan Jessee
Givanni and Rosaria Sansone
Jane Simons

Photographers
Names of photographers are followed by the page numbers on which their work appears.
Laurie A. Black: 19, 36, 38, 39, 81, 91, 93, 109
Stephen Marley: 10, 40, 47, 97
Joyce OudkerkPool: 12
Kenneth Rice: Cover, back cover, 1, 3, 4, 6, 7, 11, 21, 27, 34, 37, 54, 57, 65, 76, 79, 80, 85, 88, 104
Courtesy, Armstrong World Industries, Inc.: 8, 60, 72, 75
Courtesy, Mannington Resilient Floors: 63

Assistant for Rice Photographs
Melissa McCumiskey

Stylist for Black and Marley Photographs
Sara Slavin

Featured Work
Davidon Homes, cover and page 88
Lafayette Painting Co., page 1
Nicholas Tuosto; Diego Bros., Inc., pages 4 and 7
Jane Simons, A.S.I.D; Joan Hancock, pages 3 and 34
Cynthia Brian, Starstyle Interiors, page 6
Esther H. Reilly Interiors; Pzazz Floor Coverings, page 27
Rick Sambol, Kitchen Consultants; Jeff Kerr Construction, page 21
Dennis Buchner Design; DuPont Stainmaster Carpet by Horizon House, page 37
Ann Blair Davison, page 54
Mary Linn Coldiron; Gary Pace, page 57
Chris Volkamer, architect, page 65

Featured Work (*continued*)
Don Skogland, Viking Tile, page 76
Agnes Bourne, A.S.I.D., page 79
Charlene Martoza; Tina Martinez, Furniture Art Studio, page 80
Barbara McQueen; Sam Davis, page 85
Wasson II; Regency House, page 104

Front Cover: An elegant entry hall sets the tone for the entire house. The small square footage of most entry halls allows for special materials such as these large-format white ceramic tiles set off with contrasting spot tiles.

Title Page: A checkerboard of resilient tiles makes a colorful ground plane in this contemporary kitchen. Using the accent color for room accessories presents a coordinated room design.

Back Cover
Top left: New tile-forming technologies for slate—as seen in this kitchen—and other types of dimensioned stone have significantly lowered the cost and eased the installation process of these beautiful earthen products.

Top right and bottom left: Colorful illustrations throughout this book provide technical guidance for all stages of construction.

Bottom right: Resilient tiles are a practical and easy-to-install floor covering for laundry rooms and other heavily used locations.

Floors & Floor Coverings

SELECTION

Choosing and installing new flooring can be the most reward-
ing and dramatic part of a remodeling or redecorating project.
Although the installation itself seems to produce an instant
transformation, it is actually part of a longer process consisting of three distinct phases: selection, preparation, and
installation. This book is organized around these three phases.
You select how much of the work you choose to do yourself.

Become a flooring expert before you make the final selection.
Ask friends about the advantages and disadvantages of their
floors. Visit local floor-covering showrooms and home-
improvement stores. Compare prices. Read decorating maga-
zines and style books to get ideas. The more information you
have, the happier you will be with your final choice.

Whether you're considering wood, resilient, tile, or carpet,
the first step toward successful installation is selection. Use
the information in this chapter to get the process going.

*Different floor coverings can be used to divide a large space by function.
Large ceramic tiles set at a diagonal provide an elegant yet easy-to-clean
dining-room floor. A wood edging strip identifies the step leading down
to the cozy, carpeted living room.*

PERSPECTIVE ON FLOORS

Floors enhance the style and comfort of a house. More than any other design element, the floor sets the tone and feeling for a room. It may be the most important element in the design, or it may serve as a subtle background for furniture and collections. Adding to the challenge, a floor must also be practical, long-lasting, and appropriate.

Design Principles

Because floors are such an important part of a room, select new flooring carefully. Your concept of beauty is constantly evolving, and the simpler the floor treatment, the more flexibility you will have if you want to redecorate later on, use the room for some other purpose, or sell the house.

Usually, good design is simple design—although simplicity isn't always easy to achieve. It requires a high level of restraint, thoughtfulness in planning, and care in execution.

Light and Dark

In general, a light-colored floor will brighten a room and make it feel and look more spacious and open. Dark colors seem to contract space and make a room feel smaller. However, don't be afraid to play with these design concepts. Bending the rules could result in a room with more character and individuality.

Color

You should be aware of color terminology if you are going to discuss color possibilities with a designer. *Hue* refers to a color by name—red, blue, green, mauve. *Value* defines the relative darkness or lightness of the hue. Colors of lower value are dark, those of higher value are pale. *Chroma* refers to the saturation of a color. Strong chroma means a color that is rich and full. Weak chroma means a color with a flat look.

Trends come and go; tastes change; so approach color with

Left: A simple checkerboard pattern of resilient tile flooring visually enlarges this small laundry room. Bold floor design defines a room and should be used with care.
Opposite: A complex bordered diagonal pattern of ceramic tile forms a permanent hallway runner. The subdued colors and muted glaze of the tile keep the busy pattern from overwhelming the space.

care. You don't want to be tired of that red carpet or those black kitchen tiles after just one year.

Start the selection process by bringing home flooring samples; setting them on the floor; and looking at them in various areas of the room and in different lights. If possible, do your selection process over a number of days. Give yourself time to mull over your options.

Take this opportunity to educate your design eye. Experiment with color combinations. Don't limit your choices to your first idea. Perhaps you had your heart set on a bright blue carpet. After looking at samples on the floor, you see that a gray woven wool carpet with a subtle blue grid is easier on the eye and makes a more pleasing stage for that flowered-chintz sofa.

A dash of a favorite color on black or white or a neutral tone has a more timeless appeal than bold use of that same color. For example, a bathroom floor of white ceramic tile set off with a border stripe of turquoise tiles won't dominate the room the way a solid turquoise floor would. Experiment with patterns and look for different ways to introduce a color without making it the main attraction. On a stained-wood floor, incorporate one or more accent colors into a stenciled border pattern, for example.

Opposite: Spend as much time as necessary coordinating the colors of various elements in a room. One way to coordinate a room is to first pick a floor covering, such as this resilient sheet flooring, and then choose paint and fixtures to match.

Pattern and Scale

Scale refers to the proportional relationships among design elements. Floor patterns—whether they are flowers on a carpet, the checkered effect of tile, the lines of wood planks, or the design on resilient flooring—must be in proportion to the size and configuration of the room.

Large patterns tend to decrease the apparent size of a room. This is especially true if the pattern contains several colors. Busy patterns can be distracting, and they may make it harder to change the room in the future. An effective floor pattern need not vie for attention—it can simply provide a background for other, more flexible expressions of taste.

Small patterns are usually easier to live with than large patterns. They also provide more flexibility when it comes to designing the rest of the room. On the other hand, a minipattern can look too safe in an otherwise dramatic design. There, more adventurous patterns may be called for.

Texture

Ambience is partly a matter of texture. For instance, a stone floor in a small, dark room may feel cool and inviting in the desert states but more like a chilly dungeon in New Hampshire. When practical considerations make it necessary to use different flooring materials in adjacent rooms, it is possible to retain a unified design by

Choosing a Color

Consider these guidelines when you are deciding on a color.
- Ignore the name of the color; it can influence you more than you think.
- If you know that you want green, consider the full range of greens and think about combining different shades.
- Pay attention to an immediate response to a particular color. That impulse indicates your emotional preference.
- Narrow down your choices to three or four.
- Borrow or buy a few samples of each of your choices and take them home with you.
- Remove as many colors as possible from the room where you plan to install the floor; cover existing carpets, drapes, furniture, fixtures, etc., so that they do not influence the new colors. (Put drop cloths over surfaces that can't be removed.)
- Place the samples on the floor in the room in which they are to be installed. Look at the samples in different areas of the room. The same sample will look slightly darker on the floor than when held.
- Check the color at different times of the day and under different lighting conditions. Artificial light will change the appearance. Incandescent light adds a pinkish tone. Depending on the particular tube, fluorescent light may change the hue completely.
- Look at the samples together with paint chips and wall-covering and upholstery samples.

keeping the color consistent and just changing the texture. Use yellow ceramic tile in the kitchen, for example, and a carpet of the same or a similar yellow in the dining room. Some carpet manufacturers offer the same color in a variety of textures or weights: heavy-duty, low-loop pile for the playroom; luxurious plush for the living room; and less expensive, less durable pile for the bedrooms, where the traffic tends to be light.

Texture is a safety factor. Avoid slick surfaces at entrances and near tubs and showers; a roughened texture helps prevent people from slipping on a wet surface.

Consider the effect of texture on maintenance. Smooth-textured resilient floors are easier to keep swept and mopped than are rougher textured ones. Uniform-pile carpets show more footprints, vacuum trails, and lint than do those with uneven piles.

PRACTICAL CONSIDERATIONS

This book discusses four main types of flooring—wood, resilient materials, ceramic and dimensioned stone tile, and carpet. In choosing the right flooring for a given project, consider the principles of design. Consider practicalities as well.

Think about the nature and functional qualities of each material. Think about the location of the floor—an entrance hall is very different from a master bedroom. Think about who will be using the floor—a family with children has different needs than a single person.

Floors should be designed for the pleasure and comfort of the people who use them. The choice of flooring must also take into account budget, possible resale return on the investment, and expected use over the lifetime of the floor. When it comes to cost, choose the very best flooring that you can afford. Quality pays off in the long run.

Location is vital. Floors at entrances that get much wear and tear from walked-in dirt must be durable; but entrances give the first impression of the home, so entrance floors must be good-looking as well. Bathroom and kitchen floors must stand up to moisture from sinks and showers and must be more durable than floors in bedrooms or dining rooms. In a room that does double duty, such as a family room, some areas of the floor must withstand heavy traffic, while others should feel cozy. Parts of such a floor can be covered with area rugs and hall runners to create the cozy effect.

Maintenance is another important consideration. Given a choice most families would rather go to a picnic than stay home waxing the kitchen floor. If you have children and pets and a busy schedule, think hard about maintenance. If your heart is set on a floor that will need regular waxing, budget in the cost of a floor-polishing machine, which makes light work of this otherwise daunting task.

For heavy-traffic areas, such as entrances, halls, or kitchens, look at floorings that were originally designed for heavy-duty use in public buildings and have stood the test of time. Dimensioned stone tile is handsome and enduring; textured-vinyl tile tends to hide dirt; tough industrial carpeting is warm and muffles noise; and ceramic tile is durable and easy to care for.

Left: Although the placement of the black tiles on this kitchen floor appears random, the tiles are actually placed for their practicality in the often-used areas in front of the sink, range, and refrigerator. They resemble stepping stones across the room.
Opposite: Contrasting ceramic tiles point out the major features of this galley-style kitchen. Diagonal configurations widen narrow spaces.

PREPARATION

Proper preparation of the subfloor is the foundation for an enduringly beautiful finish floor. This chapter explains how to assess the existing floor structure and tells what steps to take before the installation begins.

Whether you install the new floor yourself or hire a professional, the preparation phase is critical. The more careful the preparation, the better the finish floor will be.

The finish floor is a relatively thin membrane. Depending on how thick or thin and how rigid or resilient it is, it will conform more or less to whatever is beneath it. The subfloor must be carefully prepared to ensure that the new floor will be properly supported, that its surface will be sufficiently smooth, that it will be protected from moisture damage, that it will move with the house, and that it will be flush with any adjacent floors.

Preparation is also essential because not every kind of flooring can be installed over every subfloor. Not all building materials are compatible with each other. Understand the requirements of your finish flooring to avoid problems later.

Coordinating the ceramic countertop tile with the ceramic floor tile gives the room a cohesive appearance. On the floor, hexagonal tiles surround small square tiles (called spots) to form a pleasing pattern.

PLANNING THE PROJECT

As with any endeavor, good planning is the key to a successful flooring installation. Whether you do the entire job yourself or hire a professional to do some or all of it, you must be responsible for accurately measuring the room or rooms so that you order the correct amount of materials.

Dealing With Professionals

Many types of professionals can help you to plan new flooring. Interior designers are trained to help with design and selection choices, and it may be well worthwhile to purchase even half an hour of their services. When you know what material you want, the next step is to decide whether to install the new floor yourself or have it done professionally.

Before approaching a dealer or installer, do some homework. The more you know about your budget, the existing floor, and what you want the new floor to look like, the easier it will be to ask the appropriate questions. Take along a dimensioned drawing of the room or rooms (see page 16).

A dealer or supplier can help to estimate the amount of material the job will require. He or she can also help to determine what preparation the existing floor may need, so be sure to describe the existing floor covering, subfloor material, and floor structure (see pages 18). Many dealers rent or lend all the tools and supplies necessary for do-it-yourself installation, or they can recommend an installer if you prefer to have the job done professionally.

Doing It Yourself

If you're accustomed to doing home-improvement projects, consider installing your own flooring. In some cases it will save time and money, although in other cases installation may be included in the price of the materials or may require considerable skill. As a general rule, the less expensive the materials and the higher the labor costs, the more you will save by doing the job yourself. The more expensive the materials or the larger the size of sheet flooring, the higher the cost of errors will be.

Estimating Materials

To estimate roughly how much material to purchase, plan to add a certain percentage to the total square footage of the room. This will ensure that there will be enough material for details, such as extending the flooring into door openings. It will also provide an allowance for error and waste.

Check the dye lots of all materials too. Dyes vary; make sure that the flooring matches perfectly across the room. Order plenty of installation materials and have all the correct tools on hand.

Do-It-Yourself or Professional Installation: Time, Money, and Skill Comparisons

This chart will help you to compare the amount of time and money as well as the level of skill required to install each type of flooring. It will help you to see what's involved in doing a job yourself or in having it done professionally. The work sheet on the opposite page will help you to itemize the details of your specific project. Use it to help determine the savings and other benefits that you might gain by doing it yourself.

	Cost of Materials	Cost of Professional Installation	Time Required for Professional Installation	Skills Required for Do-It-Yourself Installation
Wood	Moderate to high	Relatively high. May include sanding and finishing.	Time-consuming	Basic woodworking. The work is repetitive, so you get better at it as you go along. Special tools speed the process.
Resilient Flooring	Low to moderate; can be least expensive material	Relatively low. Sometimes included in the cost of the material.	Goes quickly	Installing tiles is easy. For sheet goods, accurate measuring and cutting are needed. Often takes two people to handle sheet goods without creasing or tearing.
Ceramic and Dimensioned Stone Tile	Moderate to high	Relatively high.	Most time-consuming	Careful layout and accurate tile placement are needed. Cutting requires special tools.
Carpet	Low to high; pad is extra	Relatively low to moderate. Often included in the cost of the material.	Goes quickly	Accurate measuring, cutting, and seaming are needed. Requires special tools. Often takes two people to handle heavy rolls.

Wood Strip

Sold by the square foot, strip is available in a variety of lengths, widths, and thicknesses. Add 1½ square feet for each door opening plus 3 percent if the room is fairly regular and 5 percent if it contains curves, jogs, or nooks.

Woodblock and Parquet

Also sold by the square foot, block and parquet come in boxes. Add 1½ square feet for each door opening plus 5 percent for error and waste.

Resilient, Ceramic, and Stone Tile

All tile is sold by the square foot in boxes. Add 1½ square feet for each door opening plus 5 percent for breakage. Different lots of the same tile may vary slightly in color, so check the boxes for consistency.

Resilient Sheet and Carpet

Both carpet and resilient sheet are sold by the square yard. Buy them off the roll and have them cut to length. Widths are limited: 6 feet or 12 feet for resilient sheet and usually 12 feet for carpet. Add 2 to 4 extra inches to each dimension for a safe cutting margin. If there will be seams (and their placement is crucial), add 8 to 10 percent to the total. If the room has many jogs, nooks, or bays, and if pile direction, seam placement, or pattern matching must be taken into consideration, you may have to add as much as 20 percent. Use the dimensioned drawing to consult with the dealer about these allowances.

Cost Comparison Work Sheet

To work out the details of dealer versus do-it-yourself installation costs for specific flooring materials for a room of a given size, use the form outlined here. Some of these services, such as removing furniture, should be negotiated and specially arranged with the installer.

Contractor or Dealer Charges

1. Preparation of subfloor:
   Materials $ _____
   Labor $ _____

2. Installation:
   Materials $ _____
   Labor $ _____

3. Additional Charges:
   Moving heavy furniture $ _____
   Delivery $ _____
   Finishing door openings, trim, etc. $ _____

Total $ _____

Do-It-Yourself Costs

1. Preparation of subfloor: _____ square feet of plywood or underlayment at $ _____ $ _____

2. Finish flooring materials: square feet or yards at $ _____ $ _____

3. Tools to buy (list): _____ _____
   _____ _____ $ _____
   Tools to rent (list): _____ _____
   _____ _____ $ _____

4. Supplies:
   Adhesive
   Grout or wood filler $ _____
   Nails or screws $ _____
   Sealers, stains, finishes $ _____
   Tackless strip for carpet $ _____
   Baseboards, thresholds $ _____
   Other $ _____
   _____ $ _____
   _____ $ _____
   _____ $ _____

Total $ _____

Questions to Ask the Dealer

• What are the special characteristics of the material?
• Does the manufacturer guarantee the material?
• How easy is it to maintain?
• How long is the wait for delivery?
• Does the cost of the material include installation?
• Are there any hidden costs?
• Are there any subfloor conditions that must be met before the material can be installed?
• How long will it take to install?
• Is the installation guaranteed?

Dimensioned Drawing

Whether or not you intend to do the work yourself, it's a good idea to do your own measuring and to estimate roughly how much material the project will require. Use the measurements to make a dimensioned drawing of the room. This will be an indispensable tool throughout the planning phase of your project.

• Use it as an accurate record of the size and shape of the room. Include closet and door openings and indicate the exact placement of fixed elements, such as built-in cabinets, hearths, chimneys, pipes, and floor furnace registers.

• Use it as an accurate representation of the room. A flooring materials dealer, installer, or other professional can refer to this drawing to give you advice on seaming and focal points.

• Use it to compute square footages, so that you can estimate roughly how much material the job will take and what it will cost.

• Use it as a template in planning and layout, to get the most coverage for your dollar

Measuring a Simple Space

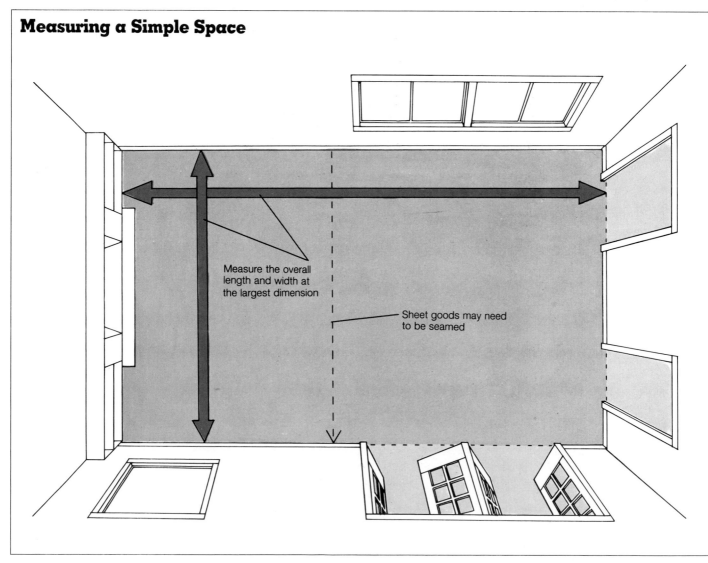

Measure the overall length and width at the largest dimension

Sheet goods may need to be seamed

investment and the most interesting finished floor for your planning time.

Rooms come in an infinite variety of sizes and shapes. Some consist of four straight walls; others have lots of nooks and jogs, built-in cabinets, closets, and so forth, all of which must be taken into account. The illustrations show two sample rooms and the measuring principles that are applicable to each. Here is one way to measure the area of a room that has built-in fixtures

1. Take the overall measurements. Measure the longest dimension of the room and then the widest dimension. Then multiply them together. For example, this room is 20 feet long and 14 feet wide ($14 \times 20 = 280$ sq ft).

2. Measure the length of each permanent feature at its base and multiply it by its width. Subtract this amount from the basic square footage.

3. Measure the length of each nook, bay, and closet and multiply it by its width. If the flooring material will extend into those areas, add this amount to the basic square footage for the extra coverage.

Questions to Ask the Installers

- Will they remove and replace the furniture?
- Will they charge for doing so?
- Will they measure the space and plan the layout?
- Will they inspect and clean the subfloor?
- How long will it take to install the flooring?
- Will they finish seams, edges, and door openings?
- Will they clean up?
- Will they dispose of old flooring?
- Will they inspect the completed installation?
- Will they guarantee the installation?

Measuring a Room With Built-ins

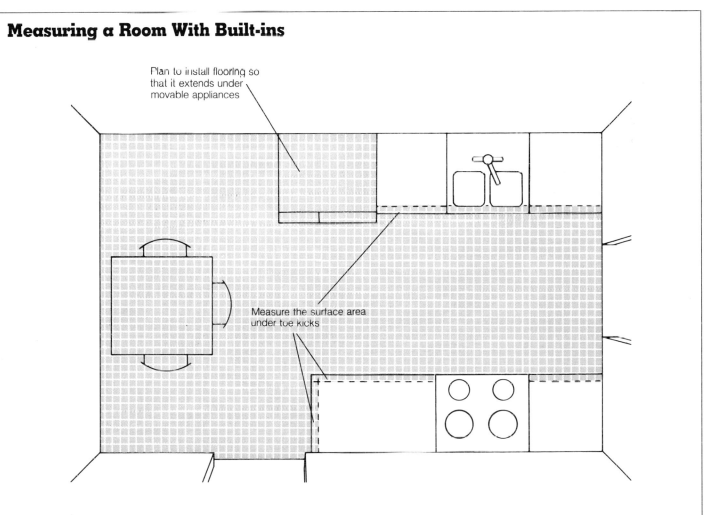

Plan to install flooring so that it extends under movable appliances

Measure the surface area under toe kicks

ANATOMY OF A FLOOR

The finish floor is essentially a skin over the real floor—that is, the structural floor that holds up the walls, furnishings, and occupants of the house and keeps out moisture and drafts. Many people never see this structural floor or understand its function.

Under the Flooring

If you are installing a new finish floor, however, you must know something about the existing subfloor, and also something about the framing, to avoid covering up problems that may affect the new floor.

Most homes are built on either a concrete slab or a wood frame subfloor. It is important to find out which one you have, because the two types are quite different. Each has specific characteristics of material and construction that will affect the new finish floor.

The floor structure is a series of layers. It is easy to see the importance of some of them. For instance, in wood frame construction the foundation and framing layers support the house, and the top layer provides the finished look. However, there is another layer, sandwiched in the middle, that also serves a critical function. This is the underlayment, and depending on the materials used for the subfloor and the finish floor, it serves one or more of several purposes. It adds rigidity to the floor. It increases its resilience. It provides a smooth surface for the flooring material and one that will accept the appropriate adhesive. It protects the floor from moisture, drafts, and dust. The discussion on page 24 and the charts on pages 43, 69, 83, and 95 will help you to determine whether the new flooring needs an underlayment, and if so, which material is best suited to your needs.

Anatomy of a Concrete Slab Floor

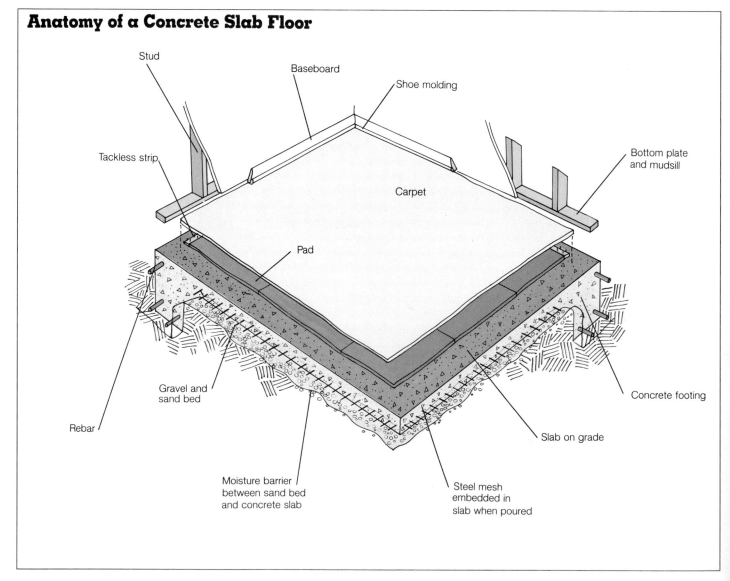

- Stud
- Baseboard
- Shoe molding
- Tackless strip
- Bottom plate and mudsill
- Carpet
- Pad
- Gravel and sand bed
- Concrete footing
- Rebar
- Slab on grade
- Moisture barrier between sand bed and concrete slab
- Steel mesh embedded in slab when poured

Note: The term *underlayment* usually refers to nonstructural material that is added just before the finish floor is installed. However, it is sometimes used to describe any layer immediately below the finish floor—even when this is the subfloor or an existing finish floor over which new flooring material will be laid. To avoid confusion be specific about what you're referring to when you discuss underlayment with a professional.

Concrete Slab Subfloors

Concrete is not a waterproof material. It retains a certain amount of moisture for months after it has been poured, and it can also wick up moisture from the ground. Therefore, special moisture barriers are often installed beneath the slab before it is poured, to prevent moisture problems that can deteriorate the finish floor. Because properly constructed concrete slabs are very strong and stable, they provide excellent backing for many types of flooring. Rigid materials, such as ceramic tile and woodblock, and flexible materials, such as resilient sheet and carpet, can be glued down to a prepared concrete slab if there is no moisture problem. Laminated wood strip is specially manufactured for glued application to concrete slab. For traditional wood strip and plank materials, a wood sleeper subfloor must be constructed over the slab to create a surface that will take nails (see page 29). If the slab is absolutely level and dry, wood flooring can sometimes be glued directly to it.

Large resilient tiles mimic the appearance of a stone floor in this living room. The neutral color of the floor covering allows many decorating choices.

Anatomy of a Wood Frame Floor

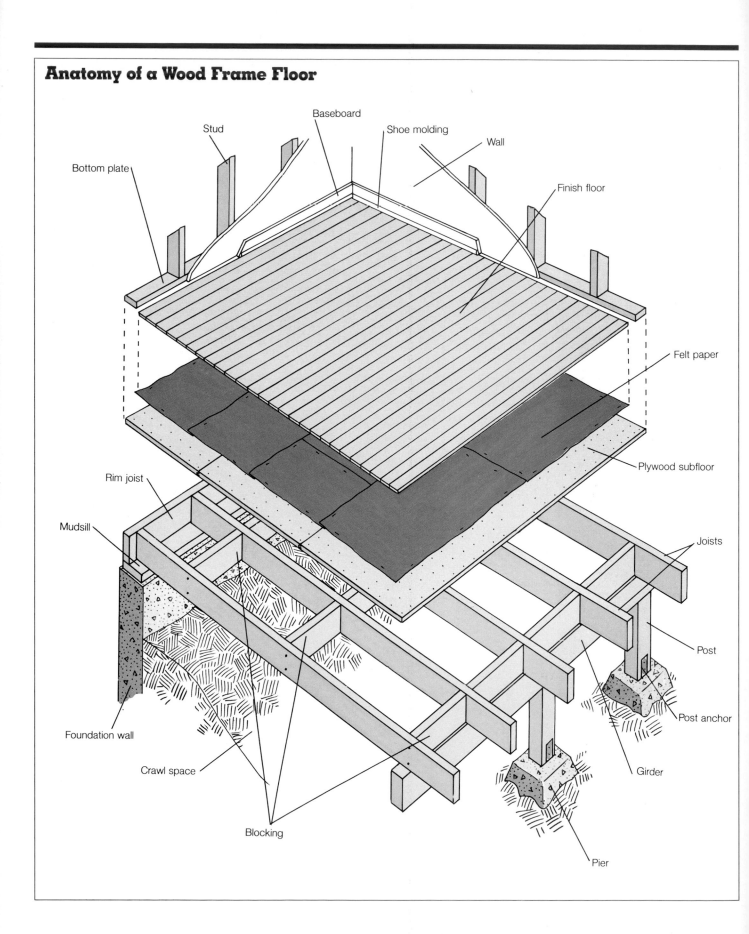

Stud

Baseboard

Shoe molding

Wall

Bottom plate

Finish floor

Felt paper

Rim joist

Plywood subfloor

Mudsill

Joists

Foundation wall

Post

Crawl space

Post anchor

Girder

Blocking

Pier

Wood Frame Subfloors

A wood frame subfloor differs from a concrete slab subfloor in several respects. It is separated from the earth, which protects it from ground moisture, but it is vulnerable to atmospheric humidity and water from spills, plumbing leaks, or roof leaks, which can cause it to warp. A wood frame subfloor is easy to nail into, and it provides a resilient base for the finish floor.

Structurally a wood subfloor is only as strong as the foundation and framing beneath it. If the foundation settles, the entire floor structure will settle, causing an uneven floor, cracks to the finish flooring, and squeaking. Repair involves jacking up the entire house and reinforcing the foundation. If you have any question about the stability of your foundation, have it checked by a structural engineer or a licensed building professional experienced with foundations before you prepare the subfloor or install new finish flooring.

Finally, it may be necessary to reinforce the joist structure to support very heavy materials, such as stone. In short, the characteristics inherent in the structural materials of the subfloor have important implications for choosing and installing the finish floor.

Just a few square feet of three types of dimensioned stone tile on this bathroom floor make a dramatic statement. Be aware that dimensioned stone tiles can be extremely heavy. Be sure to check the structural integrity of any room—especially upstairs rooms—before installing these tiles. Simple blocking between floor joists will help to support the new floor. The same effect could be achieved with ceramic or resilient tiles, which would not require a structural upgrade.

GETTING THE ROOM READY

Installing a new floor is one of the last steps in remodeling a room. If you plan to paint or to put up new wallcoverings, it's a good idea to complete these projects first. Of course, the first step in getting the room ready is to clear out the space. If the new floor is to be installed over the existing floor, that surface must be thoroughly clean and free of wax.

Doors

Make sure that the thickness of the new flooring will not interfere with the doors. If the floor will be too high for the doors to swing freely, they will have to be cut down.

To cut the bottom of a door, measure up from the existing floor a distance equal to the height of the new flooring plus ⅛ to ¼ inch. Be sure to swing the door all the way open and mark it at the highest cutoff point. Mark on the hinge pin side of the door.

Remove any doors that need cutting and any that will get in the way during the installation process. To knock the hinge pins out, tap them from below with a hammer and an 8-penny nail. If there is no access hole in the hinge barrel, set an old screwdriver or a dull chisel against the head of the pin and tap it up with a hammer.

To cut a door lay it on sawhorses with the marked side up. Holding a straightedge parallel with the bottom, mark the cutting line. Cover both sides of the line with a piece of masking tape. Cover each face of the door to prevent the saw from splintering the wood. Clamp a straight board securely to the door and sawhorse to guide the saw blade. Make the cut with a circular saw.

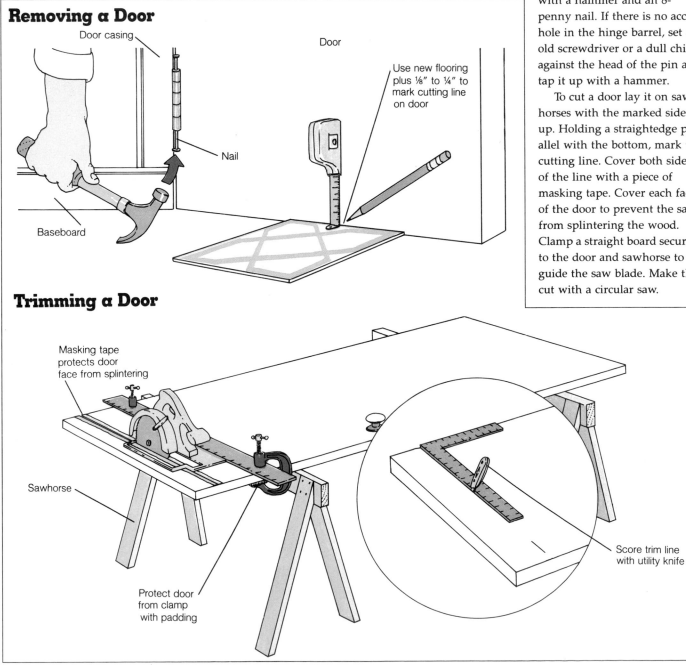

Removing a Door

Door casing

Door

Use new flooring plus ⅛" to ¼" to mark cutting line on door

Nail

Baseboard

Trimming a Door

Masking tape protects door face from splintering

Sawhorse

Protect door from clamp with padding

Score trim line with utility knife

Baseboards

New baseboards give the new floor a neat, clean look. Old baseboards should be removed if they are stained or if the material is unsuited to the new flooring. Wood baseboards rarely need to be removed, especially if you are simply replacing an old carpet with a new one. Just butt up the new carpet to the existing baseboard. This saves the cost of a new baseboard and the trouble of removing and replacing the old one. If the existing baseboards must be removed, do this before installing the new floor. The same goes for repainting the existing baseboards.

To remove a wood baseboard, hold a thin scrap of wood against the wall, wedge a pry bar between it and the top of the baseboard, and gently coax the baseboard away. If the baseboard starts to pull paint off as it separates from the wall, run a utility knife along the joint before continuing to pry. Work along the wall, prying at each point where the baseboard is nailed. Number each section as you remove it, if the baseboard will be reinstalled after the floor is laid.

To remove a vinyl cove baseboard, loosen it from the wall with a wide-blade putty knife and strip it away. Scrape the wall with the putty knife to remove any remaining adhesive.

To remove ceramic tile base borders, pop each one loose from the wall with a metal pry bar. To avoid damaging the wall, place a scrap of wood behind the bar. Scrape the wall free of any remaining grout or adhesive.

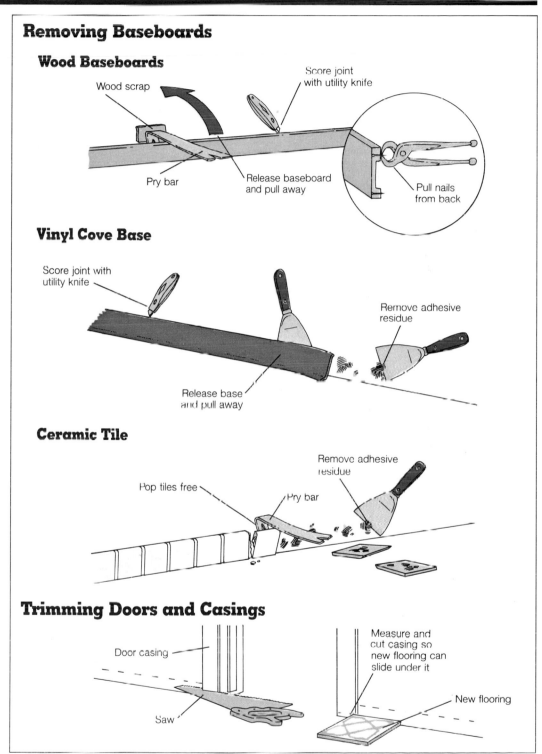

Removing Baseboards

Wood Baseboards
Wood scrap
Score joint with utility knife
Pry bar
Release baseboard and pull away
Pull nails from back

Vinyl Cove Base
Score joint with utility knife
Remove adhesive residue
Release base and pull away

Ceramic Tile
Remove adhesive residue
Pop tiles free
Pry bar

Trimming Doors and Casings
Door casing
Saw
Measure and cut casing so new flooring can slide under it
New flooring

Door Trim

The door trim, including the casings, need not be removed; they can be undercut to allow the new flooring to slip neatly underneath. To do this lay a piece of new flooring next to the casing and mark the thickness on the casing. Cut through the casing using a fine-toothed handsaw. The kerf of the blade—that is, the amount of material the teeth remove—will raise the height of the cut if you saw directly on the line. Save the line by cutting just below it.

The existing finish floor must be removed before some kinds of new materials (see charts on pages 43, 69, 83, and 95) can be installed. Use care in removing old flooring. Broken ceramic tiles are sharp. Carpet and wood are full of staples and nails.

Be Aware

Existing resilient flooring may contain asbestos fibers, which are harmful if inhaled. They are embedded in the material, but cutting, breaking, or sanding may release them into the air. Hire a professional if this material must be removed.

Old floors are dirty. Wear gloves and a dust mask when you remove an existing floor. Work carefully to avoid damaging the walls, the baseboards, or the subfloor.

Better yet, leave old flooring in place and install the new floor over it. The solid flooring is not dangerous. The asbestos can be dangerous if the old flooring is broken during removal.

Wood Flooring

Most wood strip flooring is nailed down and can be pried up with a curved wrecking bar or a flat pry bar. If there are plugs, bore them out first and remove the screws used for additional fastening. Remove any moldings and baseboards if necessary.

Insert a pry bar under the first floorboard and force it up. If there is not enough room for the pry bar, cut out a section of the first board with a circular saw. Set the blade just deep enough to cut through the finish flooring—not deep enough to cut into the subfloor below. Remove the cut section; then insert the pry bar into the opening and force up the rest of the board.

Proceed across the floor, prying up one board at a time. Work down the length of each board, placing the bar directly under the blind nailing.

If the wood flooring has been glued down, set a chisel or a pry bar against the bottom of each piece and tap with a hammer to pop it loose.

Carpet

To remove carpet installed on tackless strip, first take off all the metal edgings. Next, using a utility knife, cut the carpet into 1- or 2-foot sections. Using a screwdriver or a pry bar, raise one corner of the first section and pull it free of the strip along both walls. Release the other sections in the same way. If you want to keep the carpet in one piece, pull up one corner and work your way all around the walls.

To remove carpet installed with tacks, slide a flat pry bar under one edge and force up several tacks. Then tug hard and pull up the entire carpet, tacks and all. If that doesn't work, loosen each tack with a pry bar. Roll up the carpet and haul it away.

To remove a stapled pad, tear away as much as possible, pull up the remaining small pieces, and pry the staples from the subfloor with a screwdriver or pliers. Use a pry bar to remove the tackless strip.

To remove cushion-backed carpet that has been glued down, cut it into 12-inch strips. Pull them up one at a time, using a wide putty knife to work them free.

Scrape up any remaining chunks of foam and adhesive.

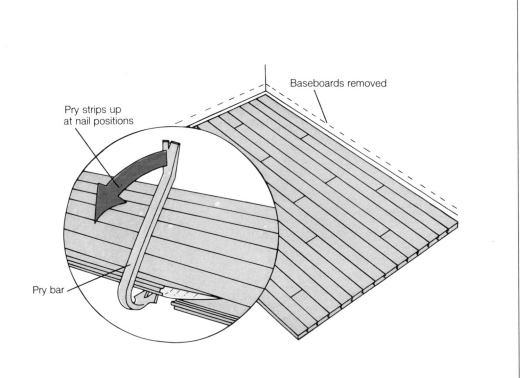

Removing Tongue-and-Groove Strip Flooring

Baseboards removed

Pry strips up at nail positions

Pry bar

If the floor must be smooth, sand off the residue with a rented floor sander or install a new underlayment.

Resilient Flooring

If sheet flooring is stapled or glued only around the edges of the room, pry up the staples or loosen the glue with a wide putty knife or a floor scraper. Roll up the sheet and haul it out of the room. If the flooring is fastened down all over, first cut it into 12- or 24-inch strips. Then work each strip free as described above. To pop off individual loose tiles, use a pry bar or a putty knife. Heat tightly bonded tiles with an iron and then pry them up. To remove any remaining adhesive, use a floor scraper or a putty knife or dissolve the residue with hot, soapy water. Some agencies rent a floor-stripping machine for removing resilient flooring.

If the flooring does not come up easily, consider taking up the underlayment as well. Use a circular saw to cut the floor into 4-foot by 4-foot sections. Set the depth of the blade to the thickness of the sheet plus the thickness of the underlayment. You will probably cut through nails, so use an old or disposable blade and wear eye protectors. Wear a dust mask too. Pry up each section of flooring and underlayment together and remove. Vacuum—do not sweep—the cleared area.

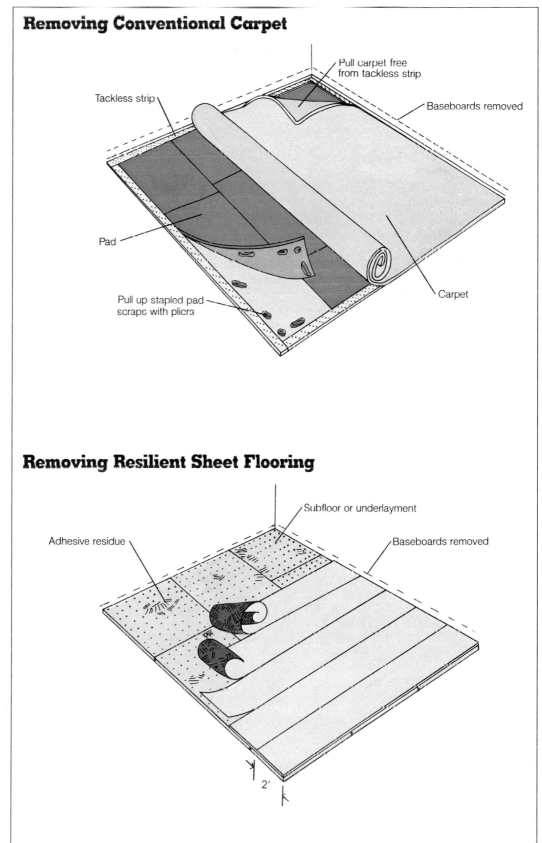

Removing Conventional Carpet

Pull carpet free from tackless strip

Tackless strip

Baseboards removed

Pad

Pull up stapled pad scraps with pliers

Carpet

Removing Resilient Sheet Flooring

Subfloor or underlayment

Adhesive residue

Baseboards removed

2'

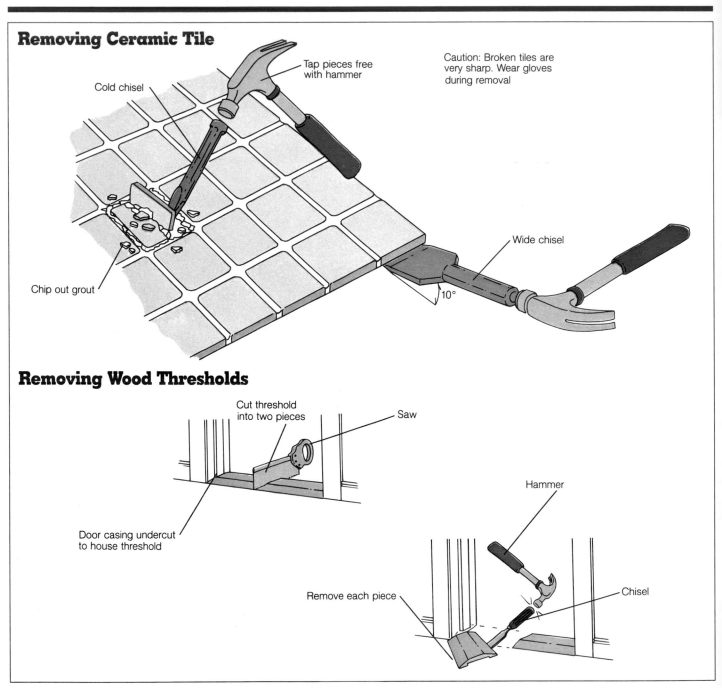

Removing Ceramic Tile

Cold chisel

Tap pieces free with hammer

Caution: Broken tiles are very sharp. Wear gloves during removal

Chip out grout

Wide chisel

10°

Removing Wood Thresholds

Cut threshold into two pieces

Saw

Door casing undercut to house threshold

Hammer

Remove each piece

Chisel

Ceramic Tile

To remove thinset installations, chip out the grout around one tile with a hammer and cold chisel. Break the tile with the hammer and remove the pieces. Then position the cold chisel under the edges of the adjacent tiles, tap to loosen, and remove them one by one. Be careful. The edges of broken tiles can be very sharp. Scrape any remaining adhesive from the subfloor.

To remove mortar bed installations, it is generally easier to force up the mortar bed itself than to break the tiles away from it. Insert a large wrecking bar or pickax under one corner of the mortar bed and pry it up from the subfloor. Use a sledge-hammer to break the bed into sections, and wire cutters or snips to cut the reinforcing mesh embedded in the mortar. Remember that carefully aimed taps are more effective than indiscriminate blows. Avoid excessive force and wear protective goggles and clothing.

Thresholds

The threshold is the covering where two floors meet. It must be removed before either floor is replaced. Pry it up from the floor with a metal pry bar. If the doorjambs were undercut to house the threshold, saw the threshold into two pieces and remove them separately.

In this study, the floor is covered with hand-painted canvas. Canvas is a suitable floor covering in rooms with light traffic. The subtle pattern and color allow the book-and-shelf patterned wallcovering to dominate the design.

PREPARING A CONCRETE SLAB

To install new flooring over a concrete slab, see the preparation guidelines indicated on the charts on pages 43, 69, 83, and 95. In many cases, it may be necessary to make surface repairs to ensure that there is an appropriately clean, smooth, even, and bondable surface for the new flooring.

Surface Repairs

To install any flooring directly on concrete, remove grease, oil, paint flakes, and dirt by scrubbing the surface well with a solution of trisodium phosphate and hot water, or use a special concrete-degreasing agent available at most hardware stores. Rinse with clear water and let the floor dry thoroughly.

Unevenness

Cracks and holes are entry points for water. If an otherwise sound floor has minor cracks or holes, widen them, clean them out, and fill them with a quick-setting hydraulic cement.

Correct uneven spots. To locate low spots, which should be filled, and high spots, which should be leveled, move a straight board across the slab and watch for gaps under it. Fill depressions with patching compound, feathering it in to the surrounding floor. To correct high spots grind them down with a rottenstone or other appropriate abrasive. If extensive smoothing is required, rent a concrete grinder, and wear a dust mask when you use it. If extensive leveling and smoothing are both required, consider using a liquid underlayment. Consult the concrete products supplier and the flooring supplier for recommendations.

Slick Surfaces

Adhesives will not bond well to a concrete floor with a slick surface. Test to see if the surface has been sealed by sprinkling water on the slab. If the water beads, the sealer will have to be removed in order to make a bondable surface. To break the sheen caused by sealers, paint, or a steel-trowel finish, sand the concrete lightly with sandpaper wrapped over a block of wood. Wear a dust mask. For very hard surfaces, you will need to scarify the floor. Machines made for this purpose are available from tool rental agencies.

Moisture Problems

Not all flooring materials must be installed over a smooth surface, but they all must be installed over a dry one. The single most common problem with on-grade and below-grade concrete slabs is that they tend to collect moisture. Several factors contribute to this problem.

Moisture can enter from outside the building. Perhaps the downspouts are not directing roof water away from the foundation line. Perhaps the earth around the building is poorly graded. In either case, water will tend to collect at the base of the house, where it is absorbed into the slab. Or perhaps there is no subsurface drainage system around the perimeter of the building. This too will cause water to collect in the surrounding soil.

All these problems are fairly easy to correct. Downspouts can be reoriented to carry water away from the slab. The earth around the house can be regraded to give a minimum slope of ½ inch to the foot so that runoff water is carried well away from the foundation. A subsurface drainpipe can be installed around the perimeter of the slab.

Some problems are more difficult to correct. Concrete, no matter how old and well cured, is a water-permeable material. Unless a moisture barrier was laid over the soil before a below-grade or on-grade slab was poured, the slab may wick up moisture from the ground.

A simple test to determine whether moisture is wicking up through the concrete is to tape a 2-foot by 2-foot square of clear plastic to the floor and leave it for one or two days. If small droplets of water form under the plastic, or if the plastic looks cloudy, there may be a moisture problem.

If there are alkali deposits on the exposed concrete surface of the slab, or if the finish flooring over the slab feels damp or looks puffy, buckled, or eroded from below, these too are danger signals. Any moisture problem should be corrected before the new finish floor is installed.

Unless you have a lot of experience with concrete,

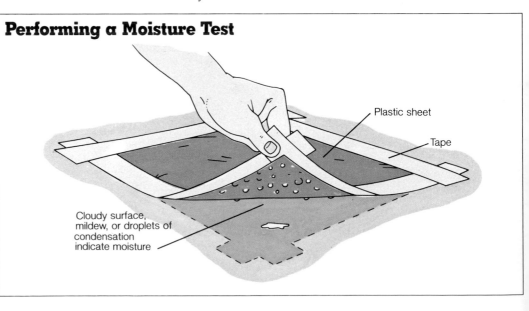

Performing a Moisture Test

Plastic sheet

Tape

Cloudy surface, mildew, or droplets of condensation indicate moisture

Wood Sleeper Subfloor Construction

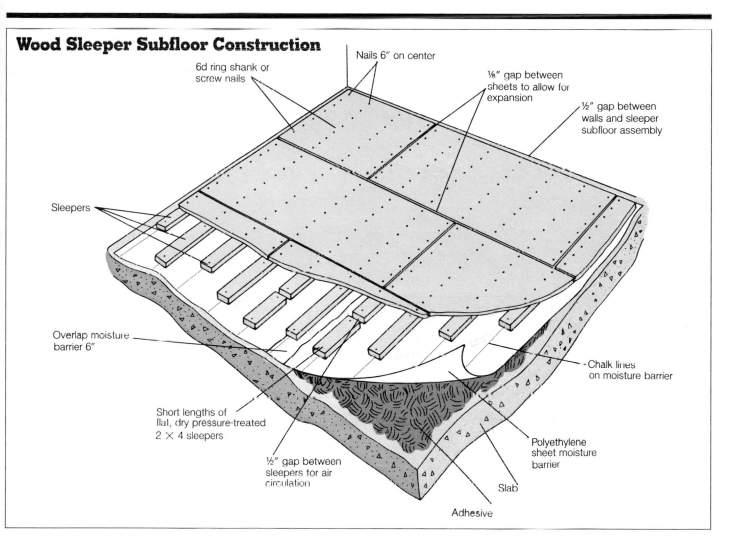

6d ring shank or screw nails

Nails 6" on center

⅛" gap between sheets to allow for expansion

½" gap between walls and sleeper subfloor assembly

Sleepers

Overlap moisture barrier 6"

Chalk lines on moisture barrier

Short lengths of flat, dry pressure-treated 2 × 4 sleepers

½" gap between sleepers for air circulation

Polyethylene sheet moisture barrier

Slab

Adhesive

---

moisture wicking up from the ground can be tricky to assess and hard to correct. You may find it worthwhile to hire a contractor who can evaluate the situation, recommend corrective measures, and carry them out if necessary.

Wood Sleepers

Wood sleepers can be installed over a concrete slab to provide a nailable surface for finish materials that cannot be fastened by other means. Wood frame subfloors also tend to be more resilient and warmer underfoot than concrete. However, not all finish materials can be installed over this type of system.

Although the instructions and the illustration show 2 by 4 sleepers laid directly on the slab, sleeper systems are sometimes constructed with up to 18 inches of ventilation space between the slab and the surface of the subfloor. This is most often done when the concrete slab suffers from serious moisture problems or surface defects that cannot otherwise be accommodated. The flooring supplier, the local building department, or a professional contractor can offer specific advice in cases of this kind.

Sweep the concrete slab clean, seal it with asphalt primer, and spread a layer of

asphalt mastic over the entire surface. The mastic should be ⅛ inch to ¼ inch thick. Lay 15-pound building paper or 6-mil polyethylene sheeting over the mastic, overlapping the edges by 6 inches. Walk over the paper or plastic to press it into place. Snap chalk lines every 16 inches across the width of the floor. Lay short lengths of preservative-treated 2 by 4s along the chalk lines. These will serve as sleepers. Leave a ½-inch to ¾-inch clearance between the ends of the sleepers and at the walls to allow for air circulation. Check the sleepers for level with a long straight-edge and shim them as needed.

Attach the sleepers to the slab with concrete nails long enough to prevent them from working loose. Install either a ⅝-inch or a ¾-inch plywood subfloor over the sleepers, leaving 1/16- to ⅛-inch gaps between the panels and a ½-inch gap at the walls. Provide underfloor ventilation to prevent musty odors or possible rot. Cut out 2-inch by 8-inch sections of the plywood subfloor along the two walls that run perpendicular to the sleepers. Make these cutouts at 6-foot intervals. Cover them with floor register grills after the finish floor is installed.

PREPARING A WOOD SUBFLOOR

Most of the preparation for wood subfloors consists of making surface repairs or installing underlayments. To remove the finish floor, see page 24. The charts on pages 43, 69, 83, and 95 outline the preparation guidelines needed for installing each of the four main types of flooring.

Surface Repairs

All surface repairs should be made before the new finish flooring is installed. Here are the solutions to several common problems.

Squeaks

Floors squeak when there is movement between two parts of their structure—for example, between the subfloor and the finish floor. The source of the squeak might be nails that have worked loose or boards that have shrunk or cupped. Locate the squeak and anchor the loose flooring with 6d or 8d nails. Spiral or ring-shank nails driven at an angle work best, since both the threads and the angle give the nails extra bite. If the squeak persists drill pilot holes and countersink wood screws through the floor into the joists below.

Cracks

It is easy to fill cracks, voids, and small depressions. Choose a filler that is compatible with any sealers or adhesives you plan to use later. Most fillers are water based or latex based. Mix them just before you use them, because they set up very fast. Clean the area of dust and debris so that the filler will adhere. Trowel the filler into the crack or depression and feather the edges with a wide putty knife. Filler dries very hard; feather it as smoothly as possible while it is still pliable. After the filled areas dry, sand them smooth and flush with the surrounding floor.

High Spots

Sand or chisel down warped boards and high spots to produce a smooth, level surface. To avoid damaging the chisel, nail the board securely first and set the nail heads. If a board is badly warped, remove that section from joist to joist, using a circular saw. If a saw will not fit into the space, drill a line of holes across each end of the defective section, break the line with a chisel, and remove the section. Chisel the remaining rough ends smooth and install a new piece of wood to match.

Slick Surfaces

Adhesives will not bond to a slick surface. If the new floor will be installed with adhesive, roughen any slick surfaces first. A light sanding using a long-handled floor or wall abrasive block works best.

Underlayments

An underlayment evens out the surface of the subfloor to provide a smooth base for the finish floor. It helps to keep out dust, drafts, moisture, and pests. It can serve to join building materials that might otherwise be incompatible, and it may provide additional structural strength.

Plywood

One good material for underlayments is plywood. Plywood is made of an odd number of thin sheets of wood (called veneers or plies) that are glued with the grains of adjacent plies running at right angles and are laminated together under pressure. It has a great deal of dimensional stability and will not warp, buckle, twist, cup, or split. Because of its inherent rigidity, plywood underlayment adds structural strength, bridges gaps, and evens out irregularities in the surface of the subfloor. It is sold in a range of grades, thicknesses, and sheet sizes.

Underlayment-grade plywood is made to satisfy the general subsurface requirements of most types of finish floors. It will hold nails and fasteners well; it has no voids between the plies; and it has smooth outer faces, since surface defects have been plugged and touch sanded.

Particleboard

Another common underlayment is particleboard. Particleboard is made of softwood chips that have been glued together and compressed into sheets under heat and pressure. It is very dense, smooth, and free of voids and knots. Most particleboard has less inherent rigidity and structural strength than plywood, though it can be used to bridge minor irregularities.

Like plywood it is sold in various grades, thicknesses, and sheet sizes. Some particleboard is made with waterproof glue. Oriented strand board (OSB) can be used as a structural subfloor.

Hardboard is a fine-fiber particleboard made from wood pulp that has been formed into sheets. It is dense, somewhat brittle, and difficult to nail, and it adds little structural strength. It comes in several sheet sizes and a limited range of thicknesses.

Tile-Backing Units

Sheets made of fiberglass and concrete are designed specifically as an underlayment for ceramic and dimensioned stone tile. Tile-backing units, also called glass mesh mortar units, provide no structural strength and should be installed over a plywood subfloor (not particleboard, which is not rigid enough to support tile). They can be used instead of a traditional mortar bed in both dry and moisture-prone areas. Tile-backing units usually come in 4-foot by 8-foot sheets. Cut them with a knife, like wallboard; nail them into place; and seal the seams with fiberglass tape. Cover nail holes with the same thinset adhesive that is used to install the tiles.

Liquids

Liquid underlayments are used to smooth, level, fill, patch, and even moistureproof subfloors. Although a few products are suitable for nonprofessional installation, most must be applied in several steps—a job best left to a skilled professional. Ask the flooring supplier about the latest products.

Preparing a Subfloor

Felt Paper Layer

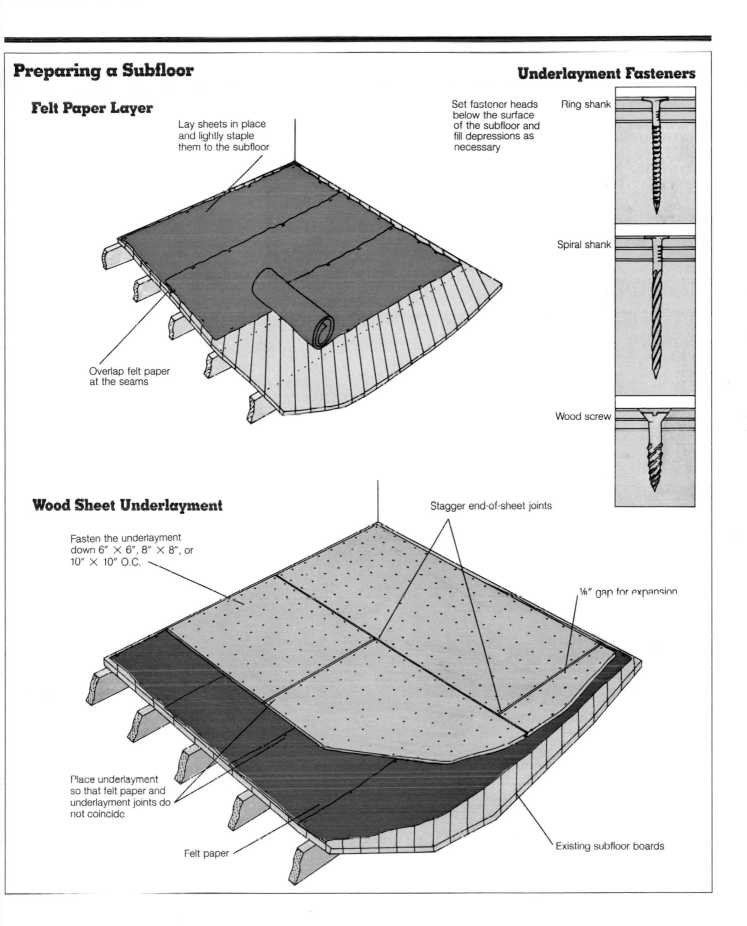

Lay sheets in place and lightly staple them to the subfloor

Set fastener heads below the surface of the subfloor and fill depressions as necessary

Ring shank

Spiral shank

Wood screw

Overlap felt paper at the seams

Wood Sheet Underlayment

Stagger end-of-sheet joints

Fasten the underlayment down 6″ × 6″, 8″ × 8″, or 10″ × 10″ O.C.

⅛″ gap for expansion

Place underlayment so that felt paper and underlayment joints do not coincide

Felt paper

Existing subfloor boards

BASIC LAYOUT TECHNIQUES

The final look of the new floor will be affected by the alignment of patterns, grout lines, wood grain, carpet pile, or other repetitive features of the material. Careful layout also ensures tight joints and well–made seams. It ensures that the last piece of material will be installed as accurately as the first.

Testing for Layout

Layout can also compensate for the fact that the room may not be square or the walls straight—that is, the flooring can mask these defects rather than exaggerate them.

Layout determines both how the finished floor will look and how smoothly the work will proceed. Considerations unique to each type of flooring material are discussed in detail in the first chapter.

In construction terminology walls are *square* if they meet at a right angle (90 degrees), that is, are precisely perpendicular to each other. Walls that are out

of square create an irregularly shaped floor. Small irregularities can be overlooked, but walls that are badly out of square can clash with lines in the flooring material. In that case, the issue becomes choosing the wall or walls to which the layout will be oriented.

Before starting the installation decide what cuts or adjustments must be made in the material. Rigid flooring won't conform to a wall that bows outward or wanders inward. If baseboards and shoe moldings won't conceal the irregularity, the material must be cut to conform to it.

Square

To determine whether the room is in square, measure the same distance from a corner down two walls. Then measure out the same distance toward the center of the room. If the two measurements are equal, the room is square and it's safe to orient the flooring parallel to any of the walls.

If not, the next step is to find which corners, if any, are square. For a quick check lay a framing square on the floor at each corner. If it fits any of the corners perfectly, measure them again with a 3-4-5 triangle (see below) to double-check.

If two adjacent corners are square, then only one of the four walls is out of square. If it is an obscure wall, square the layout to the remaining three walls. If it is a dominant wall, a focal point in the room, or a very long uninterrupted wall, square the layout to it or to an average of its orientation and that of the opposite wall.

Straight Walls

A quick way to check a wall to see whether it is straight is to measure out ¾ inch from both corners. Mark the two points and snap a chalk line between them. Any deviations between the straight chalk line and the wall will be obvious.

The 3-4-5 Triangle

The following test can be used to determine whether two intersecting lines are exactly perpendicular. Starting at the point where the two lines intersect, measure out 3 feet along one line and 4 feet along the other. Mark both positions and measure between the two marks. If the distance is exactly 5 feet, the intersecting lines are perpendicular to each other. If it is more than 5 feet, the angle is greater than 90 degrees; if the distance is less, the angle is less. For larger rooms use multiples of 3, 4, and 5 feet, such as 6, 8, and 10 foot measurements.

Methods for Layout

There are three methods of laying out a floor. The choice depends on the aesthetic effect you want to create, the unique characteristics of the flooring material, and the condition of the existing walls.

Whatever the method, test it to see what the final layout will look like before you install the flooring. Consider especially the placement of cut pieces when installing piece goods, such as tile. It's important not to lay very small pieces of flooring at the edges of the room or across high-traffic areas. Small pieces do not wear as well as larger pieces.

Checking a Room for Square

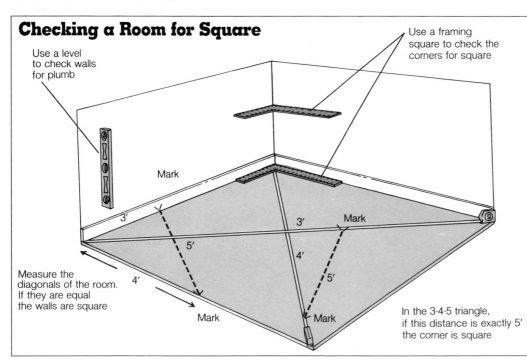

Use a level to check walls for plumb

Use a framing square to check the corners for square

Mark

Mark

3′

5′

3′

4′

Mark

5′

Measure the diagonals of the room. If they are equal the walls are square

4′

Mark

Mark

In the 3-4-5 triangle, if this distance is exactly 5′ the corner is square

Perimeter Method

The first method consists of laying out lines around the four sides of the floor, either to establish the inside edges of a border so that they will be square with the flooring field, or to keep a ceramic tile installation aligned in both directions.

Since the four walls of the room may be out of square, it is important, in laying out the lines, to keep them perfectly squared to one another rather than to the walls. The distance between the line and the wall should equal the full width of the border plus any necessary allowance for expansion space, grout lines, or irregularities in the wall.

Starter Line Method

The second method is used for installations that begin with a single course, or line of flooring, laid along one wall. It is used for wood strip and plank floors that have no border. It is easy. Simply establish a starter line at one end of the room. Align the first course of the flooring exactly with this starter line and work across to the opposite wall.

The choice of the starting wall depends on the direction in which the flooring will be installed. It also depends on aesthetic concerns such as lining up the flooring to accent a room feature like a fireplace or to make the room look longer or wider. Since the starting wall may be out of square with the room as a whole, establish the starter line by measuring back to it from a centerline drawn across the room, rather than taking measurements

from the wall itself. Because the wall and the starter line will not necessarily be parallel, the expansion gap may be wider at one end than it is at the other. If the baseboard will not fully conceal the gap, cut a tapered piece of strip flooring to fit.

If the installation includes a border, establish it using the perimeter method. Then use the starter line method to lay out and install the field.

Quadrant Method

The third method consists of dividing the floor into four quadrants and starting the installation where they meet in the center of the room. This method is used for woodblock and tile floors in which the center of the room is the visually dominant area. It is also used in rooms that are out of square or that have jogs and nooks, since it provides an accurate starting point. Finally, it is used when the tile is laid diagonally, rather than square to the room. The quadrant method makes it possible to create a symmetrical layout in any room, and to finish the installation at opposite walls with cut tiles of equal size.

Start by establishing the center point. Measure and mark the midpoints of all four walls. Snap a chalk line between each pair of opposite midpoints. The two chalk lines should be exactly perpendicular to each other. Begin the installation of each quadrant at the point where the chalk lines intersect and proceed out along each axis.

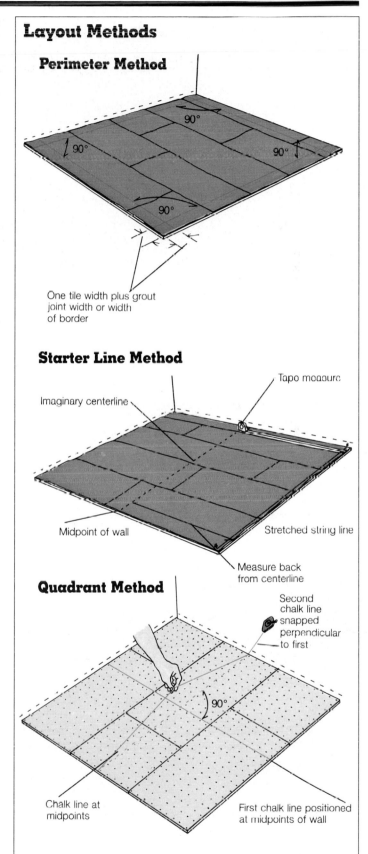

Layout Methods

Perimeter Method

One tile width plus grout joint width or width of border

Starter Line Method

Tape measure

Imaginary centerline

Midpoint of wall

Stretched string line

Measure back from centerline

Quadrant Method

Second chalk line snapped perpendicular to first

Chalk line at midpoints

First chalk line positioned at midpoints of wall

33

WOOD FLOORS

The warmth, beauty, and durability of wood make it one of the most popular flooring materials. Wood can add a special feeling of quality, permanence, and livability to any room, and it will last the lifetime of the house if it is properly installed. If it is well protected and well cared for, it will never have to be refinished but will only look better as it takes on the patina of age. Wood is also an insulating material, and its natural resilience makes it comfortable to walk on.

When it comes to design, wood is flexible as well. Wood floors work equally well in traditional and modern houses and form a perfect backdrop for all sorts of interior design motifs. They can be simply finished to show off the natural grain, or they can be stained, bleached, or painted to add pattern and character and to enhance the beauty of the wood.

Wood floors add warmth to every space they are used in, whether floor is traditionally finished. The theme of this playroom is fun: Board games have been painted onto the c trim conceals a toy train track.

CONSIDERING WOOD FLOORS

Although wood can be attractive in any area of the house, look carefully at the environmental conditions in a room for which you are considering a wood floor.

The kitchen is typically a special area where work is combined with pleasure—an easy gathering place for family and friends. Wood lends its inherent feeling of warmth and welcome to a kitchen, effectively counterbalancing the cool feeling of appliances and slick countertops and softening the hard-edged effect of cabinets.

The living room is often reserved for entertaining and may be maintained as the most formal room in the house. Yet it may be expected to perform other functions as well—those of a work space, play area, or family room, for example. Wood flooring works well in any of these situations.

Bedrooms are generally meant to be restful, to provide a feeling of calm and quiet. However, they often do double duty as hobby rooms and offices. Wood floors provide a practical and attractive background for these activities and create a pleasant feeling of ease and comfort. By installing carpeting or an area rug in the sleeping part of the room and wood flooring in the office part, it is possible to divide the space by its function. This provides a warm, cozy sleeping

Left: Alternating the direction of these large wood blocks breaks up the linear pattern wood floors often create. Wood strips can be used to emphasize certain features of a room. Use wood strips across the width of a room to make it seem wider and along the length of a room to make it seem longer. Opposite: If a wood floor is sound, refinishing is an excellent option. This hall floor was stripped and then stained using the pickling method to match the two-textured carpeted stairs. The entire procedure produced a light, airy, cohesive entrance without the work and expense of installing new floor coverings.

area and a functional, easy-to-sweep work area, all within one room.

Because bathroom floors tend to get wet, flooring must be easy to clean and moisture resistant. Appropriately finished and thoroughly sealed, wood flooring can successfully meet both requirements while providing natural ambience.

Issues of planning and design vary with the material under consideration. Linear materials, such as strip and plank, make a strong directional statement by creating lines that run either the length of the room or the width of the room. Because this directional statement is so strong, it can be used either to enhance or to alter the visual proportions of the room.

A long, narrow room will look wider and more spacious if the strips run across the width. (Check the direction of the joists, however; strip materials must run perpendicular to them.) On the other hand, woodblock or parquet tiles make no directional statement but create a very definite pattern. They can even be used to create a complex mosaic.

Both types of wood material offer a full range of detail options. The flooring field can be set off with a special, contrasting border. If that border is very wide, the flooring field becomes an area in its own right, and the border serves as a transition to it.

The profile of a baseboard as well as its height and color affect the overall feeling of a room. You can wrap the floor up the wall with a classic, high baseboard finished in the same tone as the flooring. To create a crisp, horizontal ground plane that remains distinct from the wall, use a baseboard that harmonizes with the wall color.

The tone and sheen of the finished floor also contribute to the ambient quality of the room. Dark, lustrous floors feel heavy and grounded; they tend to contract the apparent size of the space. Light matte finishes create an expansive feeling.

Left: Dark stained wide-plank flooring anchors this bedroom. Wood floors develop a patina over years of use, giving rooms a sense of history.
Opposite: A wood floor left natural (but sealed) can look both traditional and contemporary. This feature helps to balance the design of this Victorian living room furnished in a modern style. Note how the linear direction of the tongue-and-groove flooring makes the room appear wider than it actually is.

SELECTING WOOD MATERIALS

Although not all woods are specially milled for flooring purposes, many species of wood can be used for floors. The choice may depend on what is traditionally used in your part of the country—regionally produced wood is usually more readily available and less expensive than species that have to be shipped long distances.

Various grading systems are used for different species. In general, the higher the grade, the better the quality in terms of strength, appearance, regularity, and so on. However, you may prefer the knots, streaks, and spots of one of the lesser grades. Flooring is milled in several thicknesses and comes in two forms: tongue and groove, which gives a strong interlocking joint in which the nails are concealed; and square-edge, which must be nailed through the visible surface of the floor.

Some flooring materials can be purchased prefinished; the sealers and waxes are baked on at the mill. The range of species and stains is limited, however, and these materials are more expensive than most unfinished flooring.

Most people think of hardwood when they think of wood floors, although some softwoods are similarly dense and durable. *Hardwood* and *softwood* are terms that describe botanical characteristics of the wood rather than its texture or density. The softer woods do tend to dent, but you may prize their patina—the look of age and use.

Each species has a specific color range, grain pattern, texture, and density. All these characteristics contribute to the look and feel of the finished floor. In addition, of course, some woods can be stained in a wide range of tones. The chart on the opposite page lists the characteristics of various species. Use it to compare and contrast the many different woods and to get an overview of some of the many options.

The plugs in wide plank flooring can be structural, as described on page 49, or merely decorative. Either way they add hand-hewn charm to every room they grace.

Wood Flooring Materials

	Color	Grain	Texture and Density	Comments
Hardwoods				
Red oak	Tan to light pink	Highly figured	Medium density	Most popular flooring wood. Widely available. Stains and finishes well.
White oak	Light tan to yellow	Straight to highly figured	Medium density	Similar to red oak in working and finishing characteristics.
Teak	Light to dark browns and reds	Generally straight and uniform; some species have wild grain	Smooth texture; high density	Contains natural moisture resistant oils. Oil-based finishes work best.
Walnut	Reddish or chocolate brown to light tan	Straight to highly figured; burly	Hard texture; high density	Takes finish coats uniformly. Makes attractive borders and accent strips.
Maple	Light honey to near white	Fine and close	Fine texture	Extremely hard underfoot; durable. Similar to beech.
Pecan/ hickory	Honey brown to light pink	Character marked; open	Hard texture; high density	Hardest wood flooring. Species are interchangeable.
Softwoods				
Pine	White to golden	Vertical or flat; open	Low to medium density; gains patina of dents	Some pines are unacceptably soft for flooring applications.
Douglas fir	Golden orange	Flat grain wavy and open; vertical grain very straight	Flat grain variable and uneven density; vertical grain smooth and even texture	Flat grain takes stain unevenly. Vertical grain stains uniformly.
Redwood	Pink to rosy	Flat grain wavy and open; vertical grain very straight	Low to medium density; gains patina of dents	Rich, deep color when sealed. Prone to splintering.

The amount and kind of wear that the floor will receive are practical considerations that cannot be ignored. Will it be exposed to a great deal of moisture? Kitchens and bathrooms usually have high humidity, which can cause wood flooring to swell and possibly even buckle if the finish is moisture permeable. If the room has a good ventilation system, humidity probably won't affect the flooring. But if moisture tends to collect on the floor, especially in low spots, a different material might be a better option. Standing water can cause wood to stain, warp, or even rot if the surface finish can't resist it. Good installation methods and a waterproof finish such as polyurethane help to protect wood floors from these conditions.

Wood is also subject to scratches and surface abrasion. If the area where the floor will be installed collects a lot of sand or grit from traffic (in a beach house, for example), consider using a very dense hardwood topped with several coats of wear-resistant finish.

In choosing wood be imaginative but practical. Wood is one of the richest and most beautiful flooring materials; it will give you a great deal of pleasure. Take into consideration daily wear and tear, climate, and weekly maintenance, but give equal time to choosing the design and the effect that you wish to create.

PREPARING TO INSTALL WOOD FLOORING

Wood flooring will look beautiful and give years of service if it is installed over a properly prepared surface. This means that the subfloor must be structurally sound and that the surface for the new floor must be dry, relatively level, smooth, and free of dust and foreign matter.

To Begin

It is very important that any crawl space or basement below a wood floor be dry and well ventilated, because moisture causes wood floors to expand. A concrete slab subfloor must be free of moisture for the same reason, so that if the flooring is installed with adhesive, the bond will remain intact.

The chart on the opposite page summarizes the preparation steps for installing wood floors. In the presence of unique conditions, such as an extremely humid climate, restrictive floor thicknesses, or unusual specifications from the materials manufacturer, consult a professional or the local building department for recommendations.

If the chart indicates that the existing flooring must be removed, refer to the chart after you have accomplished this step to see what needs to be done to prepare the surface that is now exposed.

Storing and Handling

Wood is responsive to climatic changes, especially dampness, which makes it swell, and dryness, which makes it shrink. To keep the wood dry and ready for installation, avoid deliveries during rain or snow. For new

construction plan to have the flooring delivered after the building is closed in and all the concrete work, plaster work, and painting is finished.

After delivery store the material in the room where it will be installed. Make sure that this room is dry and heated to between 65° and 70° F. Stack the material log cabin style—or scatter it around the room so that it can acclimate to the environment—for at least five days before installation.

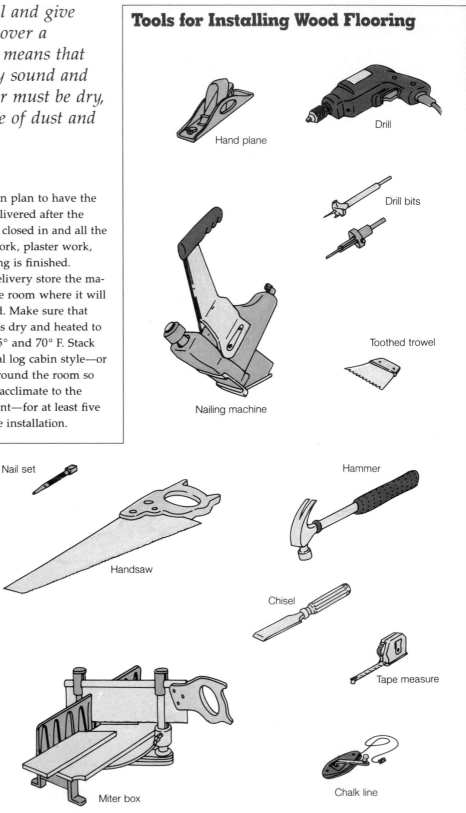

Tools for Installing Wood Flooring

Hand plane

Drill

Drill bits

Nailing machine

Toothed trowel

Nail set

Handsaw

Hammer

Chisel

Tape measure

Miter box

Chalk line

Preparation Steps for Wood Flooring Installations

This chart summarizes the preparation steps required for installing wood materials over various existing floors and floor systems. It assumes that the existing floor structure is in good condition and that any moisture problems have been corrected.

Existing Floor	Preparation for Wood Strip and Plank	Preparation for Woodblock and Parquet
Exposed Joists	• Install ¾" T&G CDX plywood subfloor. • Lay felt paper.	• Install ¾" T&G CDX/PTS plywood subfloor.
Bare Concrete	• Install wood sleeper subfloor. • Lay felt paper.	• Remove any sealer or surface finishes. • Make surface repairs to slab as needed. • Roughen the surface for best adhesion.
Wood Subfloor Over Wood Frame	• Make surface repairs as needed. • Lay felt paper.	• Make surface repairs as needed. • If subfloor is very rough or uneven or has gaps between boards, install ⅜"–½" underlayment-grade plywood or particleboard.
Over Concrete Slab	• Make surface repairs as needed. • Lay felt paper.	• Make surface repairs as needed.
Wood Finish Floor Over Wood Frame	• Make surface repairs to existing floor as needed.	• If finish flooring boards are not wider than 4", make surface repairs. Remove all surface finish. • If boards are wider than 4", install ⅜"–½" underlayment-grade plywood or particleboard.
Over Concrete Slab	• Make surface repairs to existing floor as needed.	• If finish flooring boards are not wider than 4", make surface repairs. Remove all surface finish. • If boards are wider than 4", install ⅜"–½" underlayment-grade plywood or particleboard.
Resilient Sheet or Tile Over Wood Frame	• Do not remove or sand older resilient flooring that may contain asbestos fibers. If in doubt about the flooring you wish to cover, seek professional help. • If resilient flooring is cushioned, springy, or not tightly bonded, remove it and make surface repairs as needed. • Otherwise make surface repairs to existing flooring as needed.	• If resilient flooring is cushioned, springy, or not tightly bonded, remove it and make surface repairs as needed. • Otherwise make surface repairs as needed and install ⅜" underlayment-grade plywood or particleboard.
Over Concrete Slab	• Install wood sleeper subfloor. • Lay felt paper.	• If resilient flooring is cushioned, springy, or not tightly bonded, remove it and make surface repairs to slab as needed. • Otherwise remove wax or finish and roughen the surface for best adhesion.
Ceramic Tile Over Wood Frame	• Remove existing ceramic tile. • Make surface repairs as needed. • Lay felt paper.	• If tile surface is smooth, flat, and tightly bonded, remove any wax or sealer and grind off surface sheen with a floor sander. • Otherwise remove ceramic tile. Make surface repairs as needed and install ⅜" underlayment-grade plywood or particleboard.
Over Concrete Slab	• Install wood sleeper subfloor. • Lay felt paper.	• If tile surface is smooth, flat, and tightly bonded, remove any wax or sealer and grind off surface sheen with a floor sander. • Otherwise remove ceramic tile. Make surface repairs to slab as needed.
Carpet Over Wood Frame	• Remove existing carpet and pad. • Make surface repairs as needed. • Lay felt paper.	• Remove existing carpet and pad. • Make surface repairs to subfloor as needed.
Over Concrete Slab	• Remove existing carpet and pad. • Install wood sleeper subfloor. • Lay felt paper.	• Remove existing carpet and pad. • Make surface repairs to slab as needed. • Remove sealer or surface finish and roughen the surface for best adhesion.

INSTALLING TONGUE-AND-GROOVE STRIP

Strip flooring has different names in different regions. In this book, "tongue-and-groove strip flooring" means strips 2 to 2¼ inches wide with a protuding tongue on one edge and an indented groove on the other. Narrow strips without tongue-and-groove edges are called square-edge. Wider tongue-and-groove strips are called planks.

To Begin

It takes at least basic carpentry skills to install wood flooring. This means knowing how to accurately measure, saw, and nail. Installing wood flooring also requires a good deal of stooping, lifting, and kneeling.

Consider your carpentry skills and your physical abilities before you decide to install any kind of wood flooring yourself.

The method for installing square-edge flooring is described on page 48. The method for installing plank flooring is described on page 49.

Generally strip flooring is installed perpendicular to the floor joists. However, a new wood floor installed over existing strip flooring will run perpendicular to the old flooring. If the room would look better with the strips running parallel to the joists, the subflooring must be at least ¾ inch thick and very sound.

To determine the direction and position of the joists, look at the nailing pattern of the subfloor. Because it will be necessary later on to know the exact locations of the joists, mark the center of each joist along the walls. Don't mark the floor, because it will be covered by felt paper.

Prepare the door openings. To avoid cutting and fitting the

flooring material around complicated door trim, saw off the bottoms of all casings and doorstops (but not jambs). Guide the saw with a scrap of flooring so that the blade cuts the trim exactly high enough for the flooring material to slide under it snugly. Repair the subfloor and, if necessary, mark and remove the doors and remove the baseboards (see page 23).

Note: It isn't always necessary to remove baseboards. You can simply push the new flooring snugly to the baseboard or put the new flooring close to the baseboard and cover the gap with shoe molding.

Make sure that the subfloor is clean of debris. Install 15-pound asphalt-saturated felt paper laid perpendicular to the

Laying Felt Paper

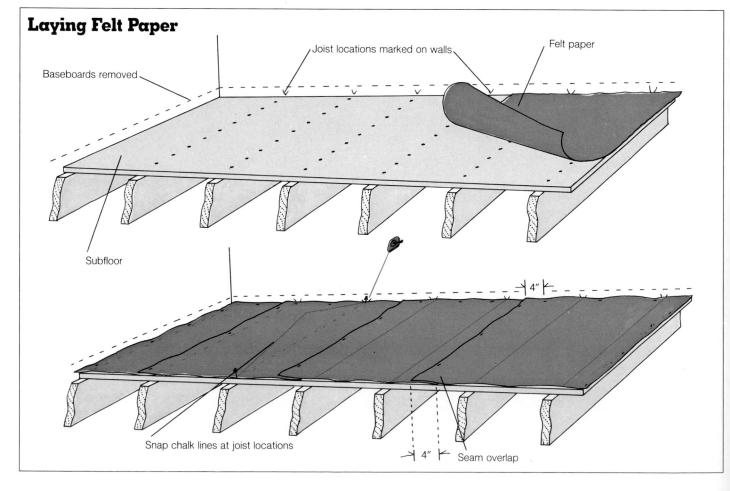

Baseboards removed

Joist locations marked on walls

Felt paper

Subfloor

Snap chalk lines at joist locations

4"

4" Seam overlap

direction of the new flooring. Overlap all edges 4 inches and neatly trim the wall ends of the paper, so that it lies flat. Staple or tack it in place, making sure that the nails or tacks are countersunk. Referring to the joist position marks on the wall, snap a chalk line onto the felt paper over the center of each joist, to guide nailing.

Next, decide which wall to use as a starting point. To make sure that the first course of flooring is properly aligned, lay down a perfectly straight line as a guide. Measure out ¾ inch at each end of the starting wall and mark both positions on the floor. Drive in a nail at each mark and stretch a string line between the nails. (The ¾-inch space, which allows for expansion, will later be covered by baseboard or shoe molding.)

Note: If the starting wall is not square with the rest of the room (check by measuring the diagonals; see page 33) use the quadrant method of layout. This technique will ensure that the floor looks square, because the flooring will register to the centerline of the room.

The Starter Course

The first row of flooring is called the starter course. Select a long, straight strip and lay it against the starter line at the left side of the room with the end ½ inch from the adjacent sidewall. (The left side is the side to your left when you stand with your back to the starting wall.) Lay the strip with the tongue edge facing into the room. The back edge should be ¾ inch from the starting wall if you are installing a new baseboard or shoe molding. If not, butt it up to the existing baseboard.

Carefully align the groove edge along the starter line. Then, beginning from the left, facenail the strip with 8-penny (8d) finishing nails into the joists and every 8 to 12 inches between them. Since face nailing can split the wood quite easily, it is best to predrill for each nail.

Next, blind-nail the tongue edge by hand. Drive nails at a 45-degree angle at every joist and at the midpoints between them. Countersink the heads with a nailset, being careful not to mar the face or tongue of the surrounding board.

Complete the starter course. Cut the last strip just short of the sidewall and use the leftover piece to start the next course. For best results use a 10-inch electric miter box saw with a carbide-tipped saw blade to make these cuts.

The Field Courses

Consider renting a pneumatic finish nailing gun, which can be set to countersink nails.

To ensure a random joint pattern in the finished floor, loosely arrange the next seven or eight courses, mixing long and short lengths. (This process is called racking the floor.) Be

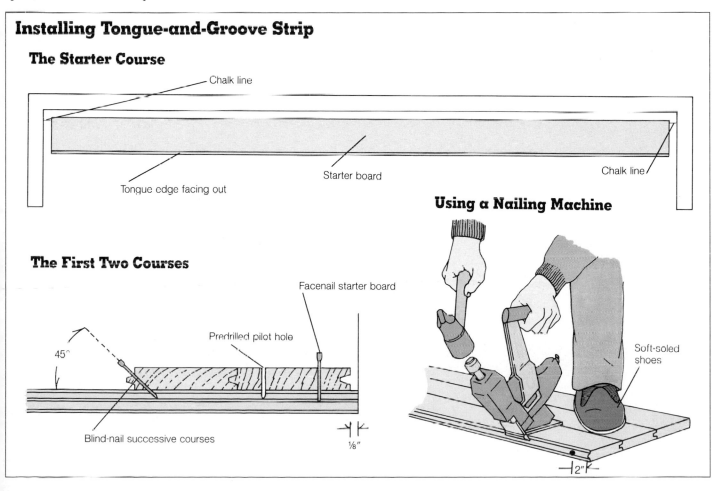

Installing Tongue-and-Groove Strip

The Starter Course

Chalk line

Starter board

Chalk line

Tongue edge facing out

The First Two Courses

Facenail starter board

Predrilled pilot hole

45°

Blind-nail successive courses

⅛"

Using a Nailing Machine

Soft-soled shoes

2"

Installing Tongue-and-Groove Strip

Staggered Joints

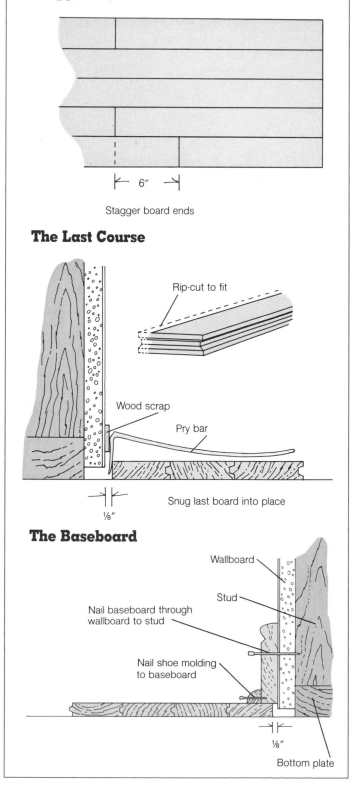

Stagger board ends

← 6″ →

The Last Course

Rip-cut to fit

Wood scrap

Pry bar

Snug last board into place

⅛″

The Baseboard

Wallboard

Stud

Nail baseboard through
wallboard to stud

Nail shoe molding
to baseboard

Bottom plate

⅛″

sure to stagger all joints at least 6 inches. Begin each course with the leftover piece from the end of the previous course.

Now hand-nail the second and third courses from left to right. Blind-nail through the tongue at each joist, at the midpoints between joists, and 2 inches from the end of each strip. Be sure every board has at least two nails in it, no matter how short it is.

Start nailing each strip 2 inches from its left end. Stand on the previously nailed courses so that your toes hold down the strip being nailed. Place the shoe flange of the nailing machine on the edge of the strip and hit the plunger with the rubber mallet, using a firm but easy swing. Continue nailing, following the same pattern used for the first three courses, always moving from left to right along each course. Keep the boards tight to ensure that they stay straight.

Special Situations

If there is a doorway for a hall or closet along the starting wall, the direction of the tongue edge will have to be reversed. To do this glue a slip tongue or spline into the groove of the starter strip. Then install the reversed courses.

If the floor has furnace register holes, posts, or other obstructions, cut and fit the flooring around them as you come to each one. In some cases, a decorative border can be framed around the obstruction. Use a miter box to cut 45-degree angles on the ends of the strips. Remove the exposed tongue by ripping the board on a table saw.

The Last Courses

As you approach the opposite wall, there will not be enough room to use the nailing gun. Blind-nail the third from the last course by hand. The last two courses must be face nailed, snugging each strip into position with a block of wood and rubber mallet.

Install the final course, butting the last strip to the existing baseboard or leaving a small gap, to be covered with new baseboard or shoe molding. It may be necessary to rip-cut strips or cut off their tongues to fill the remaining space.

Finishing Up

Install any trim before sanding and finishing the floor.

Where the two floors are of different heights, use tapered thresholds, stained and finished to match the wood flooring. Where the heights are the same, cover the joint with a flat metal strip.

Replace the baseboards, nailing them back to the wall studs. If there is a shoe molding as well, nail it to the baseboard and not to the strip flooring, so that the flooring can expand and contract freely underneath it (see page 106).

Fill cracks and nail holes in all face-nailed boards. Use a wood filler for unfinished floors and a color-matched putty stick for prefinished ones. Next, sand and seal unfinished floors (see pages 52 and 57). Prefinished floors will probably need a light cleaning and buffing to remove dirt and scuff marks caused by the installation process.

Careful attention to detail is an important part of decorating. Matching the countertop trim, cabinet door pulls, and tub surround with the dark stained tongue-and-groove floor covering produces a cohesive design in this bathroom. The wood flooring leading to the deck adds to the indoor-outdoor charm of the space.

INSTALLING SQUARE-EDGE STRIP

Square-edge flooring is less costly than tongue-and-groove because it is thinner (usually 5/16 inch), and there is less waste in milling. However, it requires face nailing and nail holes must be filled. Square-edge strip is usually 2 inches wide.

To Begin

Stretch the starter string line as described on page 45. If you plan to install a border, stretch string lines along the two side-walls and the back wall, squaring all of them to the starter line (see the perimeter method of layout, page 33).

The Strips

Install the starter course. Lay a long strip of flooring inside the starter string line, butting the plank to the baseboard if it has been left in place or leaving a ¾-inch gap at the walls if new baseboard or shoe molding will be installed to cover it. Consider renting a pneumatic finish nailing gun, which can be set to countersink nails. Predrill nail holes at both ends of the strip to prevent splitting. Keeping the edge of the strip aligned with the string line, facenail it with two 1-inch flooring nails every 7 inches. Finish the starter course.

Floor With a Border

A border is usually five or six strips deep. To install a border, lay the end wall course next. Then lay the sidewall courses to butt tightly between the starter and the end wall courses. See the illustration at right.

Install the second course, beginning with the starting wall and the left end wall. Use a miter box to cut a square end on the last piece in each course. Snug each piece firmly against the first course using a rubber mallet. Use only enough nails to hold the strip in place, but always follow the 7-inch nailing pattern. Stagger the joints. Begin each subsequent course at the starting wall, proceed to the end wall, and finish with the sidewalls.

Floor Without a Border

Working from the starter course, loosely lay out a few courses of boards and check the appearance of the joint patterns. When satisfied, snug the first piece against the starter course, using a screwdriver or a chisel as shown in the illustration at right. Nail the strips in place. When you reach the final course, you may have to rip or taper them to fit.

To keep the nailing straight, snap chalk lines or hold a long straightedge against the row that is being nailed. Set the nail heads. Cover the entire floor with filler. Sand the floor first with 80-grit, then with 100-grit, and finally with 120-grit sandpaper. Finish sanding machines are available for rent. Stain and finish as desired. Reinstall trim, if necessary.

Installing Square-Edge Strip

The Layout

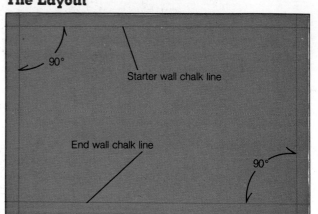

90°

Starter wall chalk line

End wall chalk line

90°

The Border

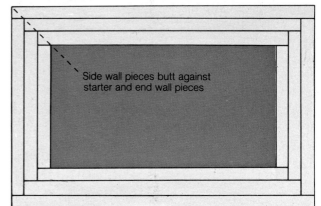

Side wall pieces butt against starter and end wall pieces

Fitting the Boards

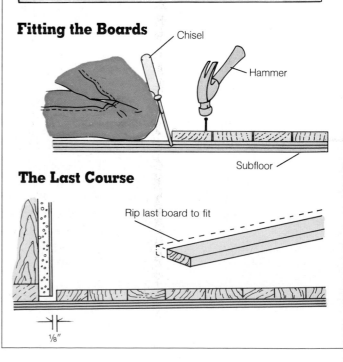

Chisel

Hammer

Subfloor

The Last Course

Rip last board to fit

⅛"

Tongue-and-groove planks are installed in the same way as tongue-and-groove strips, by facenailing the starter boards and blind-nailing the field courses (see page 45). However, do some planning first.

To Begin

Because planks come in random widths, it's important to pay close attention to the pattern they will make. Inventory the stock to see how many planks (or how much total length) you have for each width. Then plan the installation in such a way that the planks will make an attractive pattern. Be sure that there is enough of each width to lay the same pattern all the way across the floor. You don't want to run out of one size halfway through the job.

The Plugs

Some manufactured planks have wooden plugs at the ends to simulate the pegged floors of bygone days. Although some of these plugs are merely cosmetic, others actually help to hold the planks in place.

Plank flooring with real plugs is installed like other plank flooring, but think about the plug pattern first. There are several points to keep in mind. Since a plank must be cut to fit at the end of each course, these planks will have no plug holes at one end. If the leftover piece is used to start a new course, it too will have no plug holes at one end. You can counterbore the screw holes and plug them to maintain the pattern of plugs. If a new board is used to begin each course,

there will be a continuous row of plugs along the left wall. Duplicate this row along the right wall so that the edges match. To reduce the number of plugs across the edge of the floor, cut one end off the beginning board and use the leftover piece at the end of the course. Where you reduce the screw positions, blind-nail the plank securely to the subfloor.

Measure and mark the placement of the plugs at the end of each board. A 3-inch plank usually gets one plug, a 5-inch plank two, and a 7-inch plank three. For wide stock pay particular attention to the nailing schedule (see chart below); wide planks need the additional fastening.

Drill pilot holes for screws at all the marks. Counterbore them for the size of plug that you are using. (If you want plugs made of another wood that is not available from the supplier, you can cut your own with a plug-cutting bit.) Attach the flooring with No. 9 wood screws. Then glue and tap a plug into each hole. Chisel the plugs off nearly flush with the surface of the floor. They will be brought fully flush when the floor is sanded.

Install thresholds, baseboards, and other trim as needed. Sand (see page 52) and finish the floor (see page 55) for desired effect.

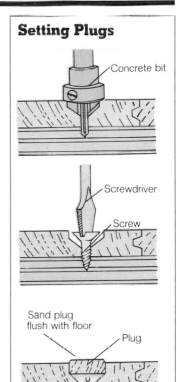

Setting Plugs

- Concrete bit
- Screwdriver
- Screw
- Sand plug flush with floor
- Plug

Nail Schedule

This chart shows the nail sizes and spacing for various wood flooring materials. For planking wider than 4 inches, No. 9 or No. 12 screws may be used for additional fastening.

Flooring	Fastener Size	Spacing
Tongue-And-Groove Flooring Blind-Nailed		
½″ × 1½″	1½″ machine-driven fastener; 5d screw, cut steel, or wire casing nail	10″ apart
⅜″ × 1½″	1¼″ machine-driven fastener; 4d bright wire casing nail	8″ apart
¾″	2″ machine-driven fastener; 7d or 8d screw or cut nail	10″–12″ apart
¾″ × 2¼″	2″ machine-driven fastener; 7d or 8d screw or cut nail	10″–12″ apart
¾″ × 3¼″	2″ machine-driven fastener; 7d or 8d screw or cut nail	10″–12″ apart
¾″ × 3″ to 8″ plank	2″ machine-driven fastener; 7d or 8d screw or cut nail	7″–8″ apart into and between joists

(If subfloor is ½″ plywood, fasten into each joist, with additional fastening between joists)

Square-Edge Flooring Face-Nailed		
5/16″ × 1⅓″	1″ 15-gauge fully barbed flooring brad	1 nail every 5″ on alternate sides of strip
5/16″ × 1½″	1″ 15-gauge fully barbed flooring brad	2 nails every 7″
5/16″ × 2″	1″ 15-gauge fully barbed flooring brad	2 nails every 7″

Source: National Oak Flooring Manufacturers Association

INSTALLING WOODBLOCK AND PARQUET

Woodblock and parquet flooring are tile materials. Use the quadrant method of layout (see page 33). If necessary, remove and trim the doors (see page 22) before installing the new flooring.

Layout

Find the midpoints of the two sidewalls and snap a chalk line between them. Snap a second line perpendicular to the first, using the midpoint of the end walls to position it. Before snapping this second line, however, square it to the first one by measuring a 3-4-5 triangle (see page 32). These preliminary guidelines may have to be moved toward or away from a wall after the test run.

If the pattern is to be laid on a diagonal, snap a second set of chalk lines at a 45-degree offset from the first. Be sure that these diagonal lines are square to each other. Make a test run and adjust the guidelines until you have a pleasing layout.

The Test Run

Begin the test layout with the quadrant that includes the doorway leading into the room. Start at the intersection of the two chalk lines and work toward both walls. At the doorway there should be a row of uncut blocks. Therefore, when the test run reaches the wall that contains the doorway, adjust it so that full blocks will end there, allowing for a ¼-inch gap along the wall. If the room has another doorway, repeat the process on an axis leading to that wall. This sets a new intersection so that any cut tiles will fall on side- or back walls. When the test run is completed, adjust the chalk lines to correspond.

Beginning Woodblock and Parquet Installations

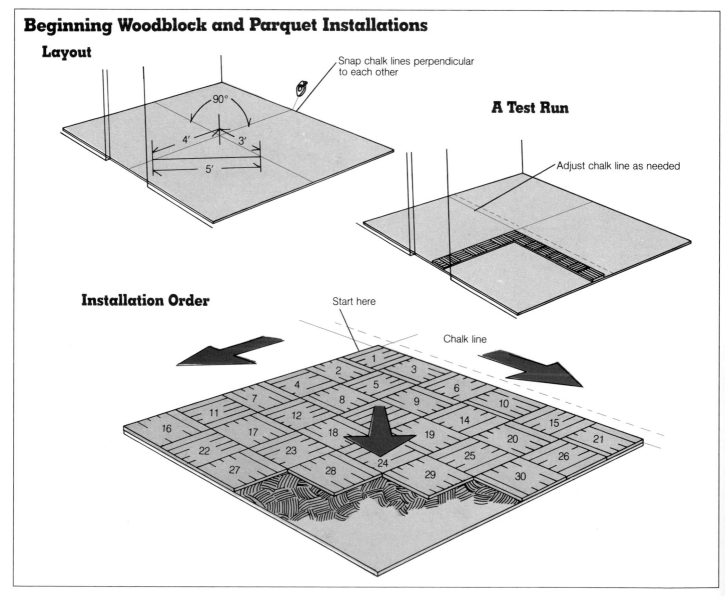

Layout

Snap chalk lines perpendicular to each other

90°

4'   3'

5'

A Test Run

Adjust chalk line as needed

Installation Order

Start here

Chalk line

Note: In most cases it is desirable to have full blocks at a doorway. However, if the resulting row of cut blocks along the opposite wall is more distracting than the cut blocks at the doorway would be, adjust the layout accordingly.

The First Quadrant

Carefully sweep and vacuum the subfloor. Apply enough adhesive for six to eight blocks at a time, or according to the manufacturer's instructions,

holding the toothed trowel at an angle of 35 to 45 degrees. If possible, avoid covering the chalk lines; otherwise, resnap them over the adhesive.

Start the installation at the intersection of the chalk lines and complete one quadrant at a time. Carefully position the first block so that it is well squared to both lines. This is the key block for guiding the entire installation. Any errors in placement will be magnified as the installation progresses,

so be careful. Lay the next few blocks along each axis, pressing each one hand-tight into place and keeping all the edges aligned. Fill in the area between the two axes, working toward the walls.

Complete the first quadrant. Continue laying blocks along each axis and filling the area in between. When you reach a wall, there should be a ¼-inch gap between it and the last tile. This gap allows the flooring to expand if the relative humidity changes. It should be filled

with a strip of cork or other compressible material to keep the blocks from shifting.

At some point it will be necessary to walk and kneel on newly laid blocks. Lay plywood over them to distribute your weight and to avoid displacing and scuffing them.

Avoid sliding the blocks into place. This forces the adhesive up into the joint, preventing a tight, clean fit. Immediately remove any adhesive that squeezes up onto the surface of the tile, using a compatible solvent. When you reach a heat register, hearth, or other obstruction, mark and cut individual blocks to fit neatly around it. Use a fine-toothed backsaw or dovetail saw for straight cuts and a coping saw or a saber saw for curved cuts. For complex shapes, cut an exact template from cardboard and trace it onto the woodblock to serve as a guide. Use the process illustrated at left for marking border tiles to fit.

The Remaining Quadrants

Follow the same process to install the other three quadrants. When all the tile has been laid, allow it to stand as long as the adhesive manufacturer specifies. Then install shoe molding and other trim, nailing it to the baseboard or the wall, not into the flooring. Install thresholds, and rehang doors, if necessary.

If the block flooring is not prefinished, sand, seal, and finish it according to the manufacturer's instructions.

Completing Woodblock and Parquet Installations

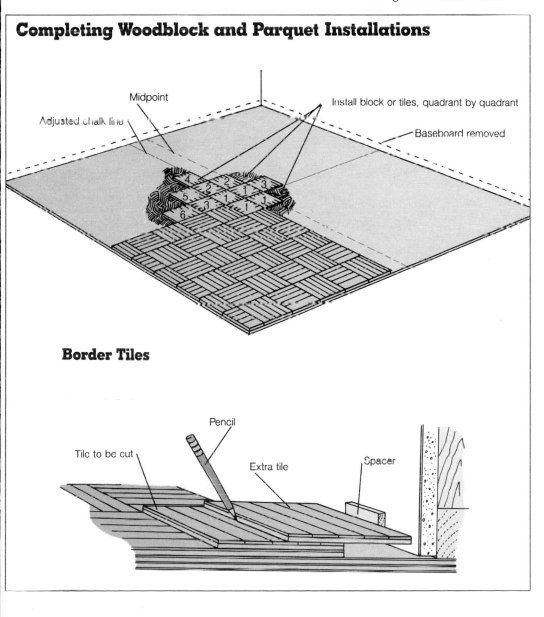

Midpoint

Adjusted chalk line

Install block or tiles, quadrant by quadrant

Baseboard removed

Border Tiles

Pencil

Tile to be cut

Extra tile

Spacer

REFINISHING OLD WOOD FLOORS

Before you decide to refinish an old wood floor, make sure that it isn't just dulled by layers of wax and grime that a good cleaning will fix.

Cleaning

To determine whether the floor needs refinishing, dip fine steel wool in kerosene or alcohol and rub in a circular motion over 1 square foot of floor. Wipe off the residue with a damp sponge, apply a layer of paste wax, and buff it up to a shine. If the results are satisfactory, you may have saved yourself a lot of trouble.

If the floor simply needs to be cleaned and rewaxed, begin by setting any protruding nails or screws and making any necessary minor repairs. Then scrub the floor with a rented buffing machine, using a steel-wool or screen pad. Pour kerosene or alcohol on one small area at a time and scrub with the machine. Pick up the residue with a damp mop (rinse often) and allow the floor to dry for several hours. When it is thoroughly dry, apply a new coat of paste wax. Apply more coats in heavy-traffic areas and buff with the buffing machine, using soft cotton pads.

Stripping

If spot repairs, cleaning, and rewaxing don't help, or if there are scratches and stains that cannot be removed, it's time to refinish. The same techniques and tools are used for all types of wood flooring.

Refinishing a wood floor is a big job, but it takes more patience and practice than special skills, and many homeowners do it themselves with great success. First, however, make sure that the wood is thick enough to sand. Remove a floor register and pry up a piece of flooring from a closet or other inconspicuous place. If the wood is less than 5/16 inch thick, it might not take another sanding.

Remove all the movable furnishings, including curtains. Cover built-in units and doorways with plastic sheeting to contain the dust. It's not necessary to remove shoe moldings and baseboards. If you choose to remove them and plan to reinstall them, mark them for later identification and take out the nails. Set any protruding floor nails 1/8 inch below the surface of the flooring.

Fill all holes and gaps. Use a wood filler that matches the color of the bare wood as closely as possible—scrape a corner to get a look at the color. Apply the filler with a large putty knife and allow it to dry thoroughly before sanding.

Tools and Equipment

Most rental agencies carry the specialized equipment required for sanding—a drum sander for the main part of the floor and a floor edger for the corners and the edges. Both are heavy-duty machines and require some strength to operate. Ask the rental agent for operating instructions; not all machines are alike. Pay attention to the procedures for changing the sandpaper, lowering the drum, and emptying the dust bags.

Purchase three grades of sandpaper: 80-grit, 100-grit, and 120-grit, in both sheets and discs. Take home plenty; most agencies won't charge for paper that you return unused. Six sheets and six discs of coarse sandpaper, eight each of medium, and eight each of fine should be sufficient for one room. The finer grits clog up more quickly. Wear a dust mask, soft-soled shoes (not black rubber, which may mark the wood), and ear protectors while sanding.

Sanding

The actual process of sanding with a drum sander is like flying an airplane, in that the takeoffs and landings are the tricky parts. The drum itself is

Refinishing Woodblock and Parquet

Filling Gaps

Sanding Sequence

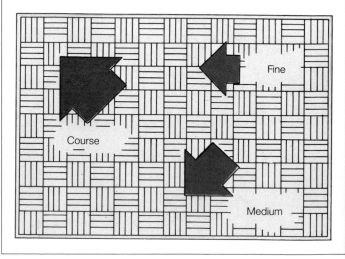

always rotating; it should be in contact with the floor only when you are pushing or pulling the machine—not while it is standing in one spot. Lower the drum to the floor as you roll the machine, and raise it up just before you reach a wall or other stopping point. Otherwise you will gouge the floor.

To begin plug the sander into an outlet in another room, in order to keep the cord out of the way. Start along the right side of the room, a few inches away from the wall and behind an imaginary centerline. Sand toward the wall. Then pull the sander back over the imaginary centerline and, overlapping the previous pass by half a drum-width, sand toward the wall again. Finish half the room in this way. Then turn around and sand the floor on the other side of the imaginary centerline

in the same manner. Always sand with the grain, unless the floor is parquet or is uneven and must be leveled.

For parquet and uneven floors, sand across the floor diagonally one way with the coarse grit, the opposite way with the medium grit, and parallel to the walls with the fine grit. Make each pass twice, first pushing the sander and then pulling it. Overlap each section half the width of the drum.

If the floor has a border with the boards laid perpendicular to the direction in which you are sanding, stop; don't sand them across the grain. Finish the main boards first. Then sand the border separately, going with the grain.

Sand the entire floor once with the coarse grit. It will become rough and fuzzy, so the next step is to smooth the wood by sanding it with the medium grit. Check and replace the sandpaper when it no longer seems to be effective. When the second sanding is complete, fill any remaining cracks or holes with filler specified for floors, spreading it with a broad putty knife. When it dries sand the floor with the fine grit.

The Edges

The drum sander cannot reach every part of the floor. Use an edger to sand along walls and in tight spaces, such as closets. The edger is a rotary sander; it uses discs. It is faster than the drum sander, but it is also more prone to gouging, and it sands across the grain. Start out in closets or other inconspicuous places until you get the feel of it. Use a scallop motion of small semicircles rather than a straight back-and-forth motion.

This helps to avoid gouging. As much as possible, avoid leaning the edger to the right or left, which forces the disc to gouge across the grain. In corners where the wood strips join at right angles, turn the edger to go with the grain, and go back and forth around that turn several times. To get at corners and other spots inaccessible to any sanding machine, use a hand scraper and finish up by hand-sanding with fine paper.

The Dust

Thoroughly clean the floor after sanding by vacuuming, buffing, and tacking. Vacuum the dust and then check again for any holes or gaps that the sanding may have uncovered. Fill them with wood putty, sand the filled areas by hand with the finest sandpaper, and then vacuum again. For best results go over the floor with a buffing machine, using fine steel-wool or screen pads. This will give a very smooth, finished effect.

Next, vacuum the floor again thoroughly to remove as much dust as possible. Then remove the final residue of dust before applying the finish. Use a painter's tack rag or a terry cloth towel wrapped around a broom and moistened with alcohol or kerosene. Wipe the corners, edges, and gaps in the floor, as well as the open spaces. Any dust left will be caught in the finish coats.

Now remove any stains. Apply ordinary household bleach in carefully controlled doses to stained areas. Rinse thoroughly and allow to dry. If necessary sand lightly again and vacuum the area that was bleached.

Refinishing Strip Flooring

Removing Baseboards

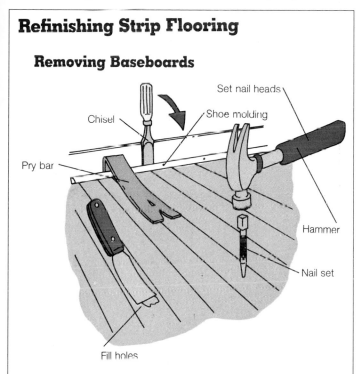

Set nail heads

Chisel

Shoe molding

Pry bar

Hammer

Nail set

Fill holes

Sanding Sequence

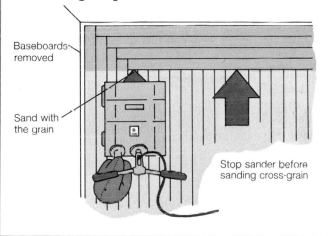

Baseboards removed

Sand with the grain

Stop sander before sanding cross-grain

CONSIDERING PAINTED FLOORS

Painting is an excellent way to give a wood—or concrete slab—floor a durable and attractive finish at a reasonable price. It is also an easy project for the do-it-yourselfer. Not only is painting practical and economical, but it offers endless opportunities for personal artistic expression.

Painted floors have a long and varied history. Today they are enjoying widespread popularity due to the durability of modern paints and finishes and a trend toward the use of handcrafted details to add richness and variety to the home. Painting a floor is a wonderful way to individualize a room or to add an element of surprise that turns an ordinary room into a showcase.

A painted floor is suitable for almost any type of room. It adds interest and excitement to a small room that might otherwise feel dull. In a formal dining room or living room, a painted floor helps to coordinate a strict design. An informal garden room, which may already feel sunny and bright, is even more vibrant with a painted floor. A painted floor adds liveliness and fun to family and playrooms. In a bedroom it can be used to create a tone of romance, childlike fantasy, or personal motif. It adds art and color to a bathroom and helps to carry out the design theme of a kitchen. A painted entrance floor is a dramatic introduction to any home.

Painted floors bring a personal touch to any room. The spring theme of this reading nook is highlighted by the ring of wildflowers painted onto canvas that has been stretched across the floor.

The range of styles and techniques here is almost endless. It includes simply painting the floor with a single color, embellishing it with a simple scene or emblem, creating surface illusions through the use of special techniques, and painting an elaborate trompe l'oeil design. If the room is decorated in a country style, paint a quilt or a needlepoint motif in the middle of the floor, or stencil a border of farm animals around the edge. For a lighter, fresher, more elegant country style, paint a floral bouquet or border on a light-colored floor. If the style is more formal, paint a restrained but richly detailed geometric pattern on the floor to simulate inlaid wood or tiles, or paint a faux finish to mimic marble or richly grained wood. If the style is contemporary, use bold geometric patterns or abstract designs. Comb painting and spatter painting are two techniques that work well for such rooms.

Painted designs can also be specific to the type of room in which they are used. Game boards can be painted on the floor of a recreation room. A woven runner can be painted down the center of a hall. If you plan to paint the floor yourself, choose a design that is well within your artistic ability. The easiest choice is probably to paint using a stencil or to copy the pattern of the wallcovering and transfer it to the floor. Otherwise ask an interior designer for the names of painters who specialize in the kind of work that you want done. Kits are also available from art suppliers for producing special effects, such as faux marble, faux granite, or wood grain.

Floor Finishes For Wood

There are so many different sealers and finishes that making a choice can be difficult. Go to a hardware store and look at the effects of various products on samples of the kind of wood you have on your floor. Read the labels to determine how to apply the finish and whether it will give you the performance you want. You may want to test the effect on an inconspicuous spot, perhaps inside a closet. The different types of sealers and finishes and their characteristics are listed below.

Penetrants
Penetrating products are absorbed into the wood and seal the pores of the grain against moisture and dirt. They include a variety of sealers, stains, and oils. Some penetrants can serve as the final finish coat, but most of them must be covered with a more durable surface finish.

Plastic sealers are commonly used on wood floors over a coloring coat. They are easy to apply, and many can simply be waxed over.

Tung and linseed oils are readily absorbed by wood and provide a soft, natural finish. Some contain color stain as well. They are easy to apply and can easily be touched up by rubbing more oil on the floor with a soft cloth. Oil finishes do not last long, and they may attract dust and dirt. Oils are not compatible with most other finishes—once you have an oiled floor, you will have to stick with it. They can be waxed with a compatible paste wax once the oil has been absorbed into the wood.

Stains add color or tone to wood while allowing the natural grain pattern to show through. A regular stain is not a finish coat, and the floor must still be sealed, oiled, waxed, or otherwise finished with a compatible product. Test the effect of the finishing coat on the color; some sealers will change the tone of the stain. Pickling stains are a mixture of paint and paint thinner. Consult the manufacturer's label for application instructions.

Stain-sealers add color or tone to the wood and semiseal it at the same time. Some provide a matte finish coat. Others must be covered with a compatible surface finish (check manufacturer's instructions) and waxed and buffed. Stain-sealers are easy to apply.

Surface Finishes
Shellac, varnish, lacquer, and polyurethane and other plastic finishes provide a hard, protective, permanent surface over color stains, paints, and sealers. They have different characteristics, but each has certain qualities to recommend it, in terms of durability, renewability, and the particular finished look it gives.

Shellac finishes are durable, though they do show scratches. Shellac goes on easily, spreads evenly, and dries quickly. It seals the pores of the wood, and it can be touched up. However, shellac resists water, heat, and alcohol poorly, and tends to have a short container life.

Varnish dries hard, withstands moisture, and can be rubbed or buffed to a high gloss. However, it is easily damaged by heat. It should be applied when the room is warm (about 70° F). Except for fast-dry varieties, it dries slowly. Thin the first coat to be applied to bare wood by 25 percent; then use it full strength for subsequent coats. Sand between coats.

Lacquer is a quick-drying, heatproof, water-resistant finish that can be rubbed to a matte or glossy luster. Lacquer can be sprayed on or applied by brush.

Polyurethane is a hard, clear, durable plastic finish that is impervious to water, alcohol, chemicals, and heat. Under normal to heavy traffic and wear, it will stay intact without chipping or cracking. It is fairly easy to apply but dries slowly, especially if humidity is high.

PAINTING A FLOOR

A stripped-wood finish floor, a wood subfloor, and a concrete slab are the most suitable surfaces for painting. You can also paint a covering, such as canvas or other durable fabric, and then cover the floor with it. Other floor coverings, such as resilient tile, resilient sheet, or ceramic tile, should be removed before painting the floor.

To Begin

Finishing a new or newly stripped wood floor is a multistep process. Floors must be properly prepared, sealed, colored, and coated. Some products take care of two steps at once. For example, some sealers contain colorants that stain the floor while closing the pores of the wood. If you are painting the floor, the priming coat will seal the floor. Whatever product you use to color and seal the floor, finish the surface by coating the entire floor with a plastic coat that will permanently protect it.

A wood floor must be structurally sound, with adequate joist support, so that the boards do not flex or sag. Secure any loose boards with nails or screws. Fill holes and any cracks wider than 1/16 inch with a floor-patching compound that can be sanded smooth after drying, such as latex-portland cement or wood filler. If any boards are cupped, sand them level or force them down with screws. Countersink the screw heads and fill the holes with patching compound. Uneven joints, which are caused by boards of different thicknesses, should be sanded level.

Sand the entire floor to bare wood, using the techniques described on page 52. Sanding removes any wax or other finishes that might prevent the paint from adhering properly, and it makes the floor smooth and level. Don't try to get the floor absolutely flawless. Paint can solve flooring problems better than most other materials, provided the floor is structurally sound, clean, and dry. Imperfections in the flooring, such as knots or thin cracks, actually add charm, as long as they do not interfere with a painted design.

Vacuum the floor thoroughly and wipe it with a tack rag. Then paint it with one coat of high-quality, oil-based exterior-grade primer.

Choosing the Paint

For the finish coats ordinary oil-based enamels and latex paints are the most readily available and offer the widest choice of colors. In general, oil-based paints create a harder film than latex. They also tend to be more forgiving of a poorly prepared surface in that they cover up most dirt and loose residue. Latex paints create a tougher, more resilient film and, because they breathe, are more suitable in damp locations, such as basements or concrete slabs.

More specialized paints are also available from many dealers.

Most manufacturers offer porch and floor paints, which are either alkyd or modified epoxy latex. The color selection is not as wide as it is for ordinary paints, but the dealer may be able to custom-mix a special color. Another durable paint is industrial enamel, which is not always available to homeowners. These enamels are tough, but they have a high gloss and they tend to be slippery. Porcelain-epoxy paints are also excellent and some of the lighter colors are available in a satin finish.

Stains, used only on wood floors, add color while allowing the grain of the wood to show. Stains are available in wood hues and in a variety of colors. The effect of coloring a wood floor with a colored stain is called pickling. Pickling stains are simply thinned paint and are applied in the same manner as regular paint.

The world of paints is always changing; it is influenced by air pollution controls, the availability of certain resources, and advances in paint

Concrete Floors

Painting is also an effective way to finish a concrete floor.

The concrete must be clean and dry. Patch cracks and uneven joints with an expansive mortar designed for such applications. Allow it to cure, following the manufacturer's instructions. If the concrete is new, wait at least 30 days for it to cure before painting.

If the floor was previously painted, check to make sure that there are no problems with flaking and peeling. Scrape off all loose or flaking paint. If such problems are extensive, remove all the old paint by scraping or stripping it with paint remover. Then scrub the floor with either tri-sodium phosphate (TSP) mixed with water according to instructions or with another general-purpose cleaning agent. Do not use dishwashing detergent—it will leave a slight film that prevents good paint adhesion. Allow the floor to dry thoroughly.

Prepare either an old or new concrete floor for painting by etching it with a solution of water and muriatic acid, which is available at most paint or hardware stores. In a plastic pail, dilute 1 part of acid with 10 parts of water. If you will be painting with a water-based paint, use phosphoric acid instead of muriatic acid, again diluting 1 part acid with 10 parts water, using a plastic pail. Be careful to follow all instructions and precautions on the container. Wear rubber gloves and goggles when working with acids.

After etching and rinsing the floor, let it dry and then vacuum up the dusty residue.

If you are using an acrylic latex paint or an alkyd porch and floor enamel, you probably will not need to apply sealer to the floor. Follow label recommendations. Once the concrete is prepared, apply the paint using the same methods as on wood floors.

technology. That is why selecting an informed paint dealer is as important as choosing the right paint. Oil-based paints, for instance, are not available in all parts of the country, and where they are available they may be high in solids and low in solvents, which could affect adherence or durability in certain applications.

Applying the Sealer

The purpose of a sealer is to close the pores of the floor. Sealers can be clear, tinted in wood hues, or even colored. Remove excess sealer that does not penetrate the wood, or it will splotch the surface.

Read the manufacturer's instructions for applying sealer. Test a scrap of wood or a spot in the back of a closet to see how many coats and how much drying time between coats give the best results. A sheepskin applicator will spread the sealer evenly without foaming it into bubbles. If you prefer to use rags, wear rubber gloves. Apply sealer sparingly, and wipe away any residue after 10 to 15 minutes.

After the sealer dries buff it with #2/0 fine steel wool. If the room is small, simply wrap the steel wool around a padded 2 by 4 and buff by hand. For a large room rent a machine. A buffing machine requires a steady hand to operate. Start in the middle of the room to avoid banging into walls until you get used to it. It will probably be necessary to change the pads once or twice, since they clog up quickly. Do the corners by hand with a scrap of steel wool. After buffing remove the dust with a vacuum and a tack rag.

Stenciling is a popular way for people who lack confidence in their artistic abilities to paint a floor. Stencils can be purchased in many art-supply stores or made by duplicating a wallcovering pattern, as shown in this bathroom.

Applying the Paint

To put color on a floor, apply stain or apply paint. It's a good idea to do this on the day that the floor receives its final cleaning, so that it won't get dirty or absorb moisture out of the air.

Single Color

Painting your floor a single color is a relatively easy project, usually easier than painting ceilings and walls. The most demanding and important part of the job is preparing the floor surface (see page 56). Allow at least a full day for preparation, more if scrubbing and drying must be repeated.

Close doors or seal off doorways to the rest of the house to prevent odors and fumes from spreading, especially when using oil-based paints (follow the manufacturer's instructions for safe use). Open all the windows in the room you are painting and turn on any exhaust fans that serve the room.

Start painting around the edge of the floor next to the baseboards with a medium-sized brush (2½ to 3 inches), not a roller; a roller can leave floor paint on the baseboards. Then paint the rest of the floor. The easiest way is to use a roller with an extension handle, but for a floor that has grooves between the boards or rough floor boards, you may have to use a brush to ensure even coverage. In either case, spread the paint evenly and work the new paint back into previously painted sections as you progress across the floor.

Allow the primer or first coat to dry according to instructions on the container, then apply the subsequent coats. The extra time and effort for painting second and even third coats is worthwhile. Paints specifically formulated for floor finishes are tough and durable and should not need further protection, but any other paints should be covered with a clear coating to ensure long life and easy maintenance.

Comb Painting

The first technique resembles children's finger painting. Comb painting consists of drawing parallel lines and swirls in abstract, repeated patterns. The comb is simply a window squeegee with notches cut out to create a zigzag edge.

After priming the floor cover it with two coats of a light-colored oil-based paint. When the second base coat is thoroughly dry, apply a top coat of a contrasting color, first mixing it in a ratio of 3 parts paint to 1 part thinner. While the top coat is wet, run the comb over it to create patterns. Experiment on scrap plywood before painting the floor itself, to test the pattern and the consistency of the paint.

Do one small section of the floor at a time. To divide the floor into permanent squares, each with its own unique pattern of swirls and lines, make a grid using masking tape laid over the second base coat. The tape should be 1½ inches or 2 inches wide, and each square in the grid should be 12 to 24 inches on a side. Apply the top coat over the tape and comb it as described above. After the top coat is completely dry, pull up the tape to expose the lines of base paint surrounding each combed section.

Stenciling

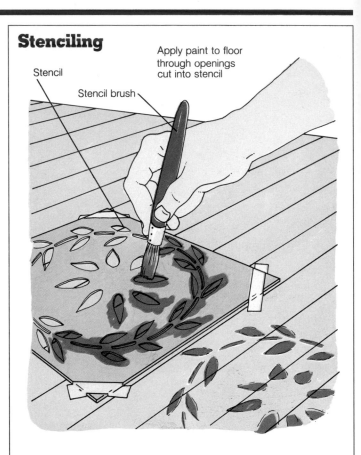

Stencil

Stencil brush

Apply paint to floor through openings cut into stencil

Comb Painting

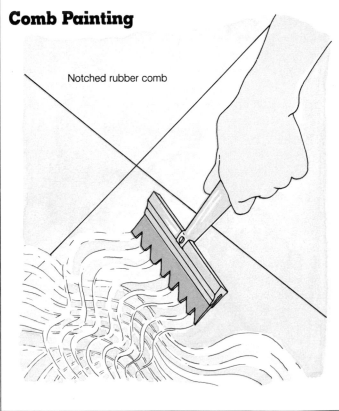

Notched rubber comb

Marbleizing

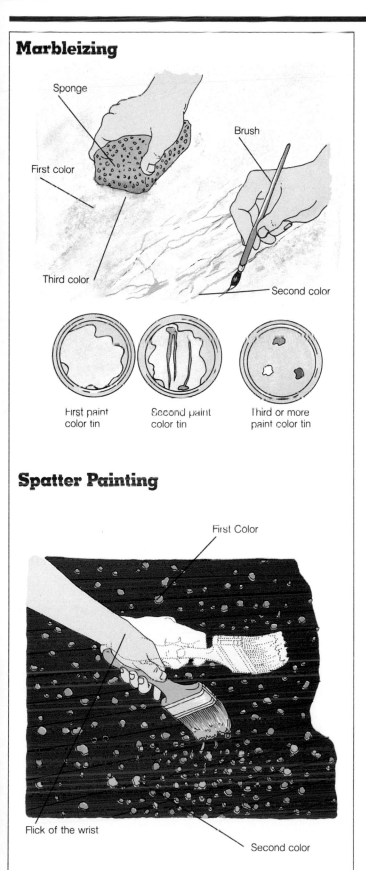

Sponge

First color

Third color

Brush

Second color

First paint color tin

Second paint color tin

Third or more paint color tin

Spatter Painting

First Color

Flick of the wrist

Second color

Marbleizing

Replicating marble and other stone requires patience and practice. Try it first on a small area or around a border. The colors must mix and run, so latex and acrylic paints generally work best.

Start by priming the floor. Then apply two coats of white semigloss latex paint. Let it dry.

Prepare two or three pie tins with various mixtures of colored paint. Kits are available or try the following recipes.

1. Thin some white latex paint and pour it into the first pie tin. Mix in a color to create a light neutral tone. Add black to get gray, or umber to get beige, for example.
2. Thin some more white paint and pour it into the second tin. Put a dab of bright-colored acrylic paint, such as red or blue, into the white paint along one side of the plate. Put a dab of another color on the opposite side. Then create veins of color on the surface of the paint by dragging a sponge applicator or a paint pad over it.
3. For more colors in the final design, place small dabs of unthinned acrylic paint in the bottom of the third pie tin.

To marbleize a section of the floor, start by brushing paint from the first plate onto the surface to create a neutral base. Immediately dip a paint pad into the second plate and drag it lightly over the wet base paint so that all the colors run together slightly. Then add more colors from the third plate with a brush, drawing it in the same direction as the paint pad. Let the colors run. Repeat the process over the entire area to be covered.

Spatter Painting

The next technique is fun and easy. Success depends more on the choice of colors than on technique. Select one color for the solid field, one for the dominant layer of spatters, and one or two additional colors for accent spatters.

Prime the floor and let it dry. Then apply one or two coats of porch and floor enamel for the solid field. When it is dry, apply the dominant spatter color by dipping a brush into the paint and flicking it at the floor. Be thorough, spatter the entire floor. An average bedroom may take half a day.

Let the floor dry at least 24 hours and repeat the process using another color. Spatter the paint more sparingly; aim for about half as much coverage as the first pass. After it dries you can add a third color, again aiming for about half as much coverage as the second pass.

The Final Coat

No matter what type of paint or stain you use, it will wear better if it is covered with two coats of polyurethane finish. This tough, clear plastic will protect even the most delicate painted design.

Polyurethane is available in spray or liquid. Apply either according to the manufacturer's instructions. The liquid types can be applied with a paintbrush or a roller (some rollers leave bubbles; a mohair one works best). Work slowly and brush or roll in the direction of the grain. Apply one coat, buff lightly with steel wool, and apply a second coat. It will dry in 8 to 16 hours. To be safe, wait 24 hours before moving the furniture back into the room.

RESILIENT FLOORS

Resilient materials—whether glossy or matte surfaced, lightly mottled or highly textured, monochromatic or marbleized— can be used to create an expansive, elegant effect in any room. They are functional and highly versatile for all areas of the house, and they provide an easy visual continuity between individual spaces or rooms.

Resilient materials are available in a wide range of colors and patterns, from subtle and refined to bold and dramatic.

Functionally, these materials create a floor that is easy to maintain, durable, and comfortable underfoot. They are practical, relatively inexpensive, and easy to install.

For bathrooms, resilient materials are an excellent choice because they are very resistant to water, are textured to prevent slippage, and can be installed quickly to minimize bathroom downtime when remodeling.

CONSIDERING RESILIENT FLOORS

When considering whether to install resilient flooring in a particular room, keep in mind both its advantages and its limitations. A major attribute of resilient flooring is that it is made to resist surface moisture.

About Resilients

Although resilient materials are deservedly popular for their no-nonsense practicality, some of them simulate expensive marble, granite, cork, or ceramic tile in a very satisfactory way. Where a beautiful visual effect comes first but practicality runs a close second, carefully chosen resilient flooring can create an atmosphere of striking elegance and refinement while keeping the budget down to earth.

These dual roles of elegance and practicality make resilient flooring a good choice for entrances. Here the floor should give a good impression to guests and yet be able to withstand the wear and tear caused by tracked-in dirt and water.

Kitchens are generally heavy-traffic, high-activity areas where soil and spills are common. When practicality and easy maintenance are important considerations, resilient materials are an excellent choice; they come in a wide variety of colors, patterns, and surface textures, and can be incorporated into almost any interior design style.

In bathrooms the cabinets and fixtures often have clean lines that convey a cool feeling. Many bathrooms benefit from the softening effects of warm-colored floors. Resilient floors come in a variety of colors to fit the style of any bathroom. The textured surfaces available on resilient flooring help prevent slipping, another important consideration for rooms where water is often spilled or moisture is evident. These include kitchens, entrances, laundry rooms, and bathrooms.

Rooms that are used to play in—children's bedrooms and family rooms—are well served by easy-maintenance resilient floors. Brightly colored tiles and sheet goods in lively patterns can add a lot of life to playroom design.

Although resilient flooring is relatively easy to install, the subfloor must be properly prepared to ensure a long wear. Most resilient materials produced today have very high-gloss finishes that bring out subsurface defects and irregularities. Unless the subsurface is properly prepared, sooner or later traffic moving through the room will abrade the finish over these irregularities and wear out the flooring. If the subsurface cannot be properly prepared, choose a different type of material.

Design Effects

Resilient materials are available that mimic natural products—ceramic tiles, pavers, cork, brick, and stone—in styles that have the look of classic linoleum, and in contemporary, nonrepresentational designs.

Linoleum has not been manufactured since the early 1970s. Modern resilient sheets are made in these classic patterns for decorative themes that harken back to an earlier age. Some styles draw on Art Deco motifs of the 1930s and 1940s. Unlike linoleum, new resilient materials are generally no-wax for easy upkeep and protection of the pattern and color.

Contemporary resilient patterns are available in neutrals and a rainbow of fashion colors. Many sheet goods are available in geometrics, others form all-over patterns that produce a smooth ground across a room. The color variety allows for a great many design choices.

When using resilient materials in any room, there are various planning and design issues to consider. These issues differ depending on whether you are using sheet goods or tile. Sheet goods generally come in 6-foot and 12-foot widths. If the room is larger than the sheet is wide, it will be necessary to seam two pieces together, and the placement of the seams will affect the look and performance of the finish floor. The continuity of sheet flooring is a special feature worth retaining. Seams can be made less visible by placing them in secondary areas of the room. A seam that runs along an existing line in the surface pattern will be essentially invisible.

Tile units offer many different design possibilities. Tiles can be laid out on a grid format oriented square to the room, or they can be laid out on a diagonal grid. The pattern can incorporate special borders, a checkerboard effect, or even a random design. The section on layout (see page 73) will help you to plan the design of a resilient tile floor.

For both sheet and tile floors, pattern, scale, surface texture, and color all contribute to the final look of the room. Pattern and scale work together to make a space feel expansive, calm, lively, busy, or cramped. Large areas can accommodate a large-scaled pattern without overwhelming the room. Small rooms, such as bathrooms, need a simple, small-scaled pattern if the floor is to create a pleasant visual effect.

Texture is often an inherent part of a repeated figure. An embossed texture in the pattern itself highlights and punctuates that pattern. The shapes that make up the figure also affect the overall feeling of the design. Curved shapes activate each other in a swirl of motion; angular shapes oppose and hold each other in place; geometric shapes interact with one another to form an integrated field. In selecting patterns, bear these principles in mind and choose the ones that harmonize with the overall design theme of the space.

Opposite: Resilient sheet is often designed to mimic other floor covering, as in this kitchen flooring, which has the grid of ceramic tiles. The lower cost, ease of care, and smooth feel of resilient flooring make it a good choice.

SELECTING RESILIENT MATERIALS

Resilient flooring materials include synthetic compounds and a few natural products, such as cork and rubber. The choice will certainly be guided by cost, but other factors will also shape the final selection. One of these will be deciding between tiles and sheet goods. Both have advantages. And, both come in a variety of pattern and color choices.

Location is an important consideration when selecting resilient materials. Some resilient materials are more resistant than others to grease, oil, water, temperature changes, denting, or chemicals. For instance, rubber is an excellent choice for a darkroom because it is especially chemical resistant. On the other hand, it doesn't resist grease and oil well, so it may not be the best choice for a kitchen. All resilient floors mold to any irregularities in the subfloor; the smoothness of the underlayment is crucial.

Once you have decided to choose resilient flooring, you must decide between tiles and sheet goods. Each type of resilient flooring has advantages. The factors to consider are aesthetic—the look you prefer—and the ease of installation.

If you plan to install the flooring yourself, check the installation instructions (see pages 68 and 73) to determine the resilient type that will best suit your room and your construction capabilities. Tiles are easy to install. Sheet goods are not much more difficult.

The chart lists the characteristics of different resilient materials. Use it to make the best selection for your particular flooring needs.

Resilient Flooring Materials

	Solid Vinyl and Cushioned Vinyl	Vinyl Composition	Rubber	Vinyl-Coated Cork
Color, Pattern, and Texture	Wide range of colors and patterns. May be laminated with fabric, wood, or marble chips. Smooth or embossed surfaces.	Many colors and patterns. Solid and marbleized colors. Smooth or embossed surfaces.	Handful of solid and marbleized colors. Smooth, ribbed, or studded surfaces.	Limited range of natural cork colors. Smooth surfaces.
Durability	Grease and oil resistant. Susceptible to heat. Cushioned vinyl may dent. Medium- to heavy-duty gauges.	Good for damp areas, properly seamed. Good resistance to chemicals. Light-, medium-, and heavy-duty gauges.	Good for damp areas. Very good resistance to most chemicals. Susceptible to grease and oil stains. Heavy-duty gauges.	Grease and oil resistant. Susceptible to heat. Cushioned vinyl may dent. Medium- to heavy-duty gauges.
Resiliency	Cushioned materials are very comfortable underfoot. Good sound insulation.	Not as resilient or sound insulating as solid vinyl.	Very comfortable underfoot. Good sound insulation.	Very comfortable underfoot. Good sound insulation.
Maintenance Requirements	Use water-based products only. Damp mop; avoid excess water.	Use water-based products only.	Use water-based products only. Requires frequent polishing.	Use water-based products only. Damp mop; avoid excess water.
Relative Cost	High.	Low to medium.	Medium to high.	Highest.

Opposite: The use of different flooring helps to divide a large space. Resilient strips, patterned to resemble wood, are a practical choice in the food preparation area, and black dimensioned stone tiles dress up the adjacent eating area.

PREPARING TO INSTALL RESILIENT FLOORING

Resilient flooring is manufactured in light gauges, and because it has no inherent structural strength it will conform to the surface on which it is laid. Cracks in the subfloor, voids in the underlayment, even small depressions from nail heads will show through the finish floor and make it subject to uneven wear, which reduces its durability.

To Begin

If the subfloor or the existing floor is not perfectly smooth, install a new subsurface of underlayment-grade plywood before laying the resilient flooring.

Resilient materials must be installed over a perfectly dry surface. Small amounts of subsurface moisture may evaporate harmlessly through wood or carpet, but a resilient floor acts as a moisture barrier. Moisture that collects underneath resilient flooring can force up the adhesive bond. In humid climates choose a waterproof and stable underlayment material.

The chart on the opposite page summarizes the preparation steps for installing resilient floors. It assumes that the existing floor is in good condition and that any moisture problems have been corrected.

In the case of unique conditions, such as an extremely humid climate, refer to the installation specifications from the manufacturer.

If the chart indicates that the existing flooring must be removed, refer to the chart after you have accomplished this step to see what needs to be done to prepare the surface that is now exposed.

Storing and Handling

Avoid storing resilient tiles or sheet flooring in areas subject to freezing or fluctuating temperatures. Sheet flooring needs to "relax." Unroll it in a room heated to 70° F for at least 24 hours before installation. It is easiest to unroll sheet flooring in the room where it will be installed. Once it has relaxed, reroll it with the face side in before measuring and cutting.

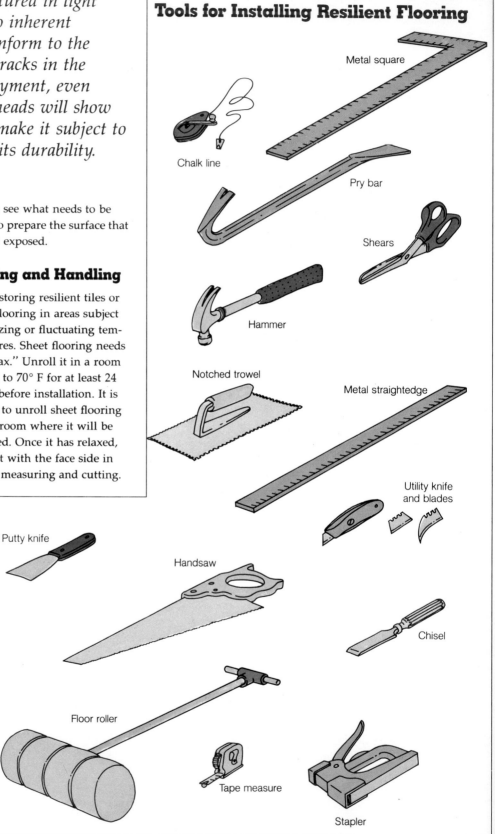

Tools for Installing Resilient Flooring

Metal square

Chalk line

Pry bar

Shears

Hammer

Notched trowel

Metal straightedge

Utility knife and blades

Putty knife

Handsaw

Chisel

Floor roller

Tape measure

Stapler

Preparation Steps for Resilient Flooring Installations

This chart summarizes the preparation steps required for installing resilient materials over various existing floors and floor systems. Install new flooring over the existing floor whenever possible.

Existing Floor	Preparation for Resilient Sheet or Tile
Exposed Joists	• Install ¾" T&G CDX plywood subfloor. • Install ⅜"–½" underlayment-grade plywood. • Fill joints and nail or screw head depressions and sand surface smooth.
Bare Concrete	• Make surface repairs to slab as needed.
Wood Floor or Subfloor	
Over Wood Frame	• Make surface repairs as needed. • Install ⅜"–½" underlayment-grade plywood. • Fill joints and sand surface smooth.
Over Concrete Slab	• Remove all wood materials to expose the slab. • Make surface repairs to slab as needed.
Resilient Sheet or Tile	
Over Wood Frame	• Do not remove or sand older resilient flooring that may contain asbestos fibers. If in doubt about the flooring you wish to cover, seek professional help. • If the resilient flooring is cushioned or springy, remove it and make surface repairs as needed. • If the resilient flooring is embossed, is not tightly bonded, or has wax or surface sheen, install ⅜" underlayment or underlayment-grade plywood. • Fill joints and sand surface smooth.
Over Concrete Slab	• Do not remove or sand older resilient flooring that may contain asbestos fibers. If in doubt about the flooring you wish to cover, seek professional help. • If the resilient flooring is cushioned, springy, or not tightly bonded, remove it and make surface repairs to slab as needed. • If the resilient flooring is embossed, smooth the surface with a liquid underlayment. Otherwise remove wax and roughen the surface for best adhesion.
Ceramic Tile	
Over Wood Frame	• If possible, remove existing tile. Otherwise smooth and even out the surface with a liquid underlayment. • After removing existing tile, make surface repairs to exposed subfloor as needed. • If subfloor is very rough, install ⅜"–½" underlayment-grade plywood. Fill joints and nail or screw head depressions and sand surface smooth.
Over Concrete Slab	• If possible, remove existing tile. Otherwise smooth and even out the surface with a liquid underlayment. • After removing existing tile, make surface repairs to slab as needed. If surface is very rough or uneven, smooth it with a liquid underlayment.
Carpet	
Over Wood Frame	• Remove existing carpet and pad. • Make surface repairs to subfloor as needed. • If subfloor is very rough, install ⅜"–½" underlayment-grade plywood. Fill joints and sand surface smooth.
Over Concrete Slab	• Remove existing carpet and pad. • Make surface repairs to slab as needed.

INSTALLING RESILIENT SHEET FLOORING

It is not difficult to install resilient sheet, but the work is physically demanding. You must be prepared to lift and carry full rolls—and the rolls are heavy.

To Begin

Measuring and cutting must be absolutely accurate, or the entire sheet will be wasted. Professionals can install resilient flooring quickly—and are prepared to do the heavy lifting and the accurate cutting. Balance the cost of their labor against your own strength and skill before you decide to do this job yourself.

Start by preparing the surface of the existing floor (see page 67). It is generally best to replace all the baseboards or the shoe molding. This makes installation easier because the edges of the sheet needn't be perfectly straight, since the new molding will cover them, and it gives the finished floor a cleaner line. If you plan to reuse the existing baseboards or shoe molding, mark the pieces for later identification.

Make sure that all the doors will clear the new flooring (see page 22). If they will not, measure, mark, remove, and trim them now.

Measuring and Cutting

There are two ways to measure resilient flooring, using a template and trimming to fit. Whichever method you use, double-check all measurements. Cut the flooring to size using a utility knife, shears, or a rotary power cutter.

The sheet material comes in 6- and 12-foot widths. It should be unrolled and allowed to relax at room temperature for several hours before cutting (see page 66).

For measuring and cutting, roll the sheet out, face up, on a clean, flat surface, such as a well-swept driveway or garage floor. Do not assume that the factory edges are straight or that they are square to the pattern, if there is one. Check the edges with a straightedge or snap a chalk line and measure from that. Use a water-soluble felt-tip pen or grease pencil for marking glossy surfaces.

Using a Template

One method of measuring and cutting is to use a template, or large pattern. To make it, cover the floor with 15-pound felt or other building paper, overlapping the seams 2 inches and taping them together. The edges of the template should be within ½ inch or so of the walls, cabinet bases, and other obstacles. The template does not have to be a perfect fit. To keep the paper from shifting around, cut out small holes every 3 or 4 feet and stick a piece of masking tape over each one.

When the pattern is in place, scribe a line around the perimeter, using a steel straightedge held against the wall. This line will be a guide for holding the straightedge when you cut the sheet flooring. After scribing a line around the entire room on the pattern, carefully roll it up.

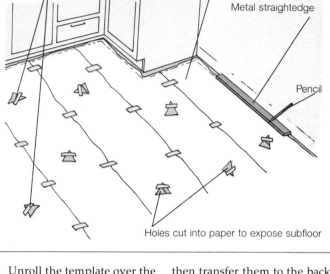

Measuring Template

Tape · Paper pattern · Metal straightedge · Pencil

Holes cut into paper to expose subfloor

Unroll the template over the material. If the flooring material has a pattern in it, such as simulated tile with grout lines, be sure the template lines up with the pattern lines so that these lines will not look awkward in critical places such as doorways or along prominent walls. Tape the template down the same way here as it was taped to the floor. To guide the cutting knife, use the same straightedge as you used for scribing the line around the perimeter. Hold the straightedge against the line and cut along the outer edge. After cutting, discard the pattern (or save it for the next time you will replace the floor), roll up the resilient sheet, and carry it to the room. This method will provide a perfect fit, and no flooring will be wasted.

Trimming to Fit

The second way to measure and cut is to measure the dimensions of the room, mark them on a rough sketch, and then transfer them to the back of the flooring. The measurements must be extremely accurate. Include any permanent features, such as built-in cabinets or a hearth. Starting from the longest edge of the longest wall, begin marking out the measurements. Double-check each one. Add a 3-inch allowance to all edges. This excess allows for adjustment before the final trimming.

Roll up the flooring, face inside, so that the longest edge of the longest wall remains on the outside. Carry it into the room and position that edge so that its margin (if there is one) curls up the wall. Unroll the sheet, tugging and adjusting it so that it is essentially centered and the pattern lines are square to the room. Make relief cuts at the outside and inside corners of the margin as you proceed. Do this very carefully, slitting the corners just enough so that the margin opens to let the sheet lie flat. Be careful not to cut beyond the margins. To fit around a pipe or post, cut a slit from the edge closest to the obstruction. Adjust the flooring around the object by making small relief cuts. When it fits trim it exactly.

It may be necessary to trim twice, first to remove most of the margin and second to perfect the fit. Begin by making freehand cuts with a utility knife. Feel along the edge of the floor with the knife blade or use a straightedge pushed tightly against the fold of the margin. Cut as you go, leaving a ⅛-inch gap along the wall to allow for expansion. The gap will later be covered by baseboard or cove molding.

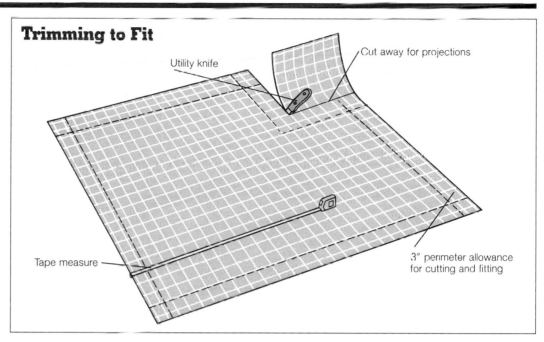

Trimming to Fit

- Utility knife
- Cut away for projections
- Tape measure
- 3" perimeter allowance for cutting and fitting

Adhesives for Resilient Flooring

Different adhesives are used for different types of flooring and different kinds of subfloor. They are classified according to the categories listed below. Follow the manufacturer's instructions carefully and use caution with flammable adhesives. The room should always be well ventilated. Avoid using equipment with electric motors that may cause sparks, and do not smoke. Make sure that all pilot lights are off.

Adhesive	Flooring Material	Subfloor	Comments
Water-Soluble Paste	Vinyl materials with rubber backing, cork, vinyl cork (not solid vinyl, asphalt, vinyl-composition)	Concrete or wood above grade	Must be rolled.
Asphalt Based (asphalt emulsion, cut-back asphalt)	Asphalt, vinyl-composition	Concrete or wood above, on, or below grade	Do not mix with water for on- or below-grade floors.
Latex Adhesive	Solid vinyl, vinyl-composition, rubber, cork, linoleum	Concrete or wood above, on, or below grade	Good for moisture situations; dries quickly. Keep from freezing. Wear rubber gloves.
Alcohol-Resin	Vinyl, rubber, cork, linoleum	Concrete or wood above grade	Not entirely waterproof. Flammable.
Epoxy Cement	Solid vinyl, rubber tiles	Concrete or wood above, on, or below grade	Good for perimeter and seam sealing; high strength; must be mixed. Wear rubber gloves; provide ventilation.
Cove Base Cement (solvent based)	Vinyl and rubber cove base	Above grade	Flammable. Wear rubber gloves; provide ventilation.
Synthetic Rubber Cement	Vinyl cove base, metal nosings and edges (not asphalt, vinyl-composition)	Any wall	Flammable. Provide ventilation.
Neoprene Adhesive	Vinyl and rubber stair treads, nosings, corner guards	Any wall	Water-resistant. Flammable. Provide ventilation.

Proceed carefully around the room, making sure that the sheet doesn't move. At doorways without thresholds, trim the flooring at the centerline of the closed door.

Gluing

Some kinds of sheet come complete with a band of adhesive around the perimeter and under the seams. Others can be installed with staples set so close to the edges that the base trim will hide them. However, some sheet materials must be glued down all over.

To apply adhesive, carefully lift up half of the sheet and fold it back onto the other half. Spread the adhesive on the floor with a toothed trowel, following the manufacturer's directions. Work from the corners to the center of each length of wall. Special applicators are available for hard-to-reach spots. Unfold the sheet back down into place and walk on it to press it into the adhesive. Repeat the process for the other half of the sheet.

Finally, use a mallet and a padded block to press the flooring into the adhesive around the edges, or, if adhesive was spread over the entire floor, use a roller. You can rent one from a tool rental outlet or from the flooring dealer. Start at the center and roll toward the edges to bond the new flooring fully.

To completely finish the project, replace the trim (see page 106). Install either the baseboards or the shoe molding, making sure to drive the nails into the wall rather than into the flooring, or a vinyl cove base. Install thresholds and rehang the doors.

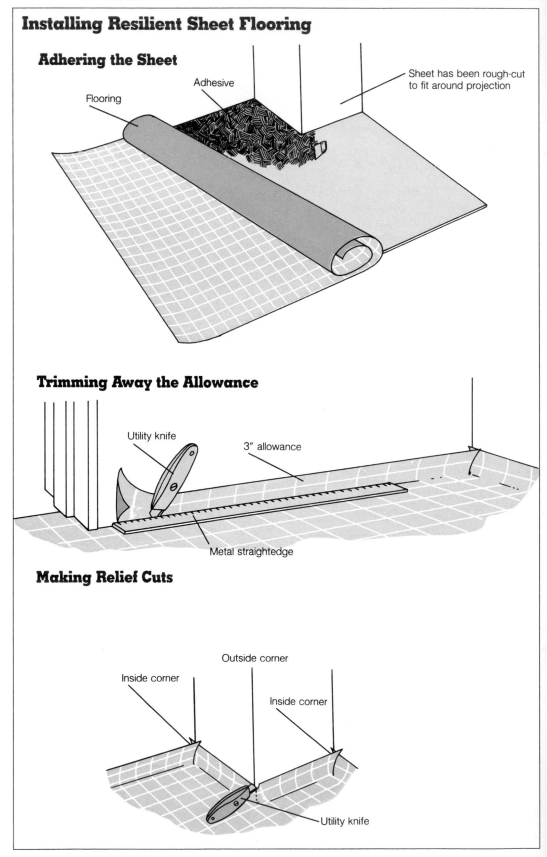

Installing Resilient Sheet Flooring

Adhering the Sheet

Flooring
Adhesive
Sheet has been rough-cut to fit around projection

Trimming Away the Allowance

Utility knife
3" allowance
Metal straightedge

Making Relief Cuts

Outside corner
Inside corner
Inside corner
Utility knife

Seaming Resilient Sheet Flooring

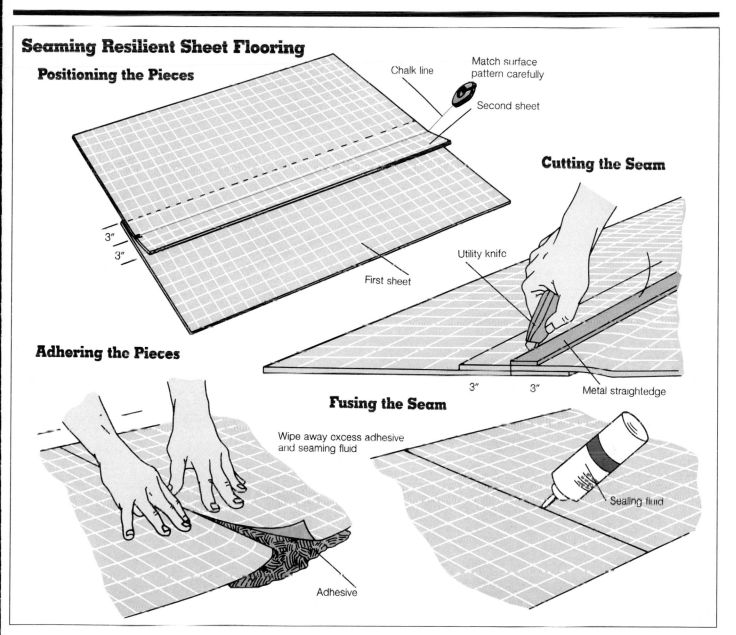

Positioning the Pieces

Chalk line

Match surface pattern carefully

Second sheet

3"
3"

First sheet

Cutting the Seam

Utility knife

3"   3"   Metal straightedge

Adhering the Pieces

Fusing the Seam

Wipe away excess adhesive and seaming fluid

Sealing fluid

Adhesive

Seaming

If it is necessary to seam two sheets of resilient flooring, use the following procedures. First, establish the best location for the seam. It should be in an inconspicuous, low-traffic area. Cut out, fit, and trim the first sheet, leaving a 3-inch margin along the edge to be seamed. Glue (or staple) this sheet in place, stopping 8 or 9 inches short of the actual location of the seam.

Next, cut and fit the second sheet. It should overlap the seam edge of the first sheet by 3 inches. Be sure to align the two sheets so that the pattern, if any, matches perfectly. Apply adhesive to the floor, stopping 5 or 6 inches short of the edge of the first sheet. Press the second sheet into place, leaving its unglued edge overlapping the first sheet.

To cut the seam use a chalk line or a straight line in the flooring pattern for a guide.

Run a sharp utility knife against a steel straightedge, carefully cutting through both layers of flooring.

Remove the scrap pieces. Glue down the seam by pulling back both edges of flooring and spreading a band of adhesive along the floor. Then join the two edges together and press the seam into the adhesive. Immediately wipe off any adhesive that oozes up between the pieces and clean the seam with a compatible solvent.

After the adhesive has set up for the time specified by the manufacturer, seal the seam with a special solvent that melts the edges enough to fuse them together. The solvent comes in a bottle that includes a special applicator spout. Run the spout along the seam, following the directions on the label. Apply the sealer only to the seam, not to the flooring, to make the seam waterproof.

Creative options abound when two-toned resilient tiles are used to form patterns, as on the floor of this music room. To try this idea at home, first check with a flooring retailer for the component systems available to you. Then measure your floor area and draw it proportionately on large-scale graph paper. Test your ideas by drawing combinations of tiles on the paper.

INSTALLING RESILIENT TILE

Just about anyone can install resilient tile. It requires few special tools, and the materials are not particularly expensive; if you goof, it's not the end of the world. Toss the tile and grab a replacement.

To Begin

The following instructions apply to resilient tiles without adhesive backing. Peel-and-stick tiles are even easier to install; just follow the manufacturer's directions. Floor preparation and layout are the same in both cases.

Before beginning the installation, sweep and clean the subfloor. It is not necessary to remove the baseboard; you can butt the new tiles right up to it. However, it is usually best to replace the baseboard with vinyl coving after the new flooring is in place. This makes installation easier, since the coving will cover the edges of imperfectly cut tiles.

Layout

If the room is irregular or contains many built-in protrusions, lay out the guidelines on the largest rectangular portion of the floor.

Measure and mark the midpoints of the two opposite side walls and snap a chalk line between them. Then do the same for the two end walls, but before snapping the second chalk line, be sure that it is squared to the first. To check for square use the 3-4-5 triangle (see page 32) and adjust the chalk line accordingly.

To lay out a diagonal pattern, first establish guidelines as illustrated below. Then measure 5 feet out along each axis from the intersection and make a mark. Find the midpoints between these marks. Snap a chalk line through two opposite midpoints. It should intersect the center at a 45-degree angle to the original quadrant lines. Extend this line in both directions to the walls. Now snap a chalk line across the remaining two midpoints. Make sure that this second diagonal is perfectly squared to the first. Make any necessary adjustments.

Next, test the layout. Lay dry tiles along both axes of one quadrant, starting at the center and working toward the walls. If the space between the last tile and the wall is less than the width of half a tile, adjust the centerline to make it at least that wide. Continue testing layouts with dry runs until the borders have a satisfying look. For the sake of durability and appearance, borders that front an opening or a doorway should have full tiles.

The First Quadrant

Thoroughly sweep and vacuum the floor. Read the instructions on the label for the open time. This is the period during which tile can be laid before the adhesive becomes too dry to make a good bond. The open time is different for different products. For some adhesives you'll have enough time to set only six or seven tiles. For others you'll have enough time to set most of a quadrant in one application.

Adhesive is most commonly applied with a notched trowel in two steps, spreading and then combing. Notched trowels come in a variety of sizes. Use the size recommended by the adhesive manufacturer. Begin in the center of the room and spread a small amount of adhesive into one quadrant, being careful not to cover up the chalk lines. Use the smooth side of the trowel to spread the adhesive in one pass. Avoid spreading it too thick, which will cause it to ooze between the tiles, or too thin, which will prevent a good bond. Then use

Layout Methods

Straight Layout

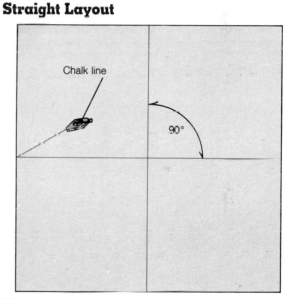

Chalk line

90°

Diagonal Layout

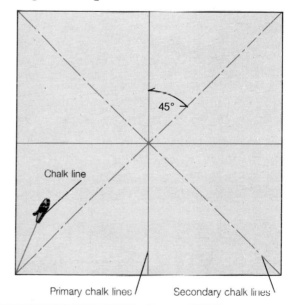

45°

Chalk line

Primary chalk lines   Secondary chalk lines

the notched side of the trowel to comb the adhesive. Allow it to become slightly tacky before setting the tiles.

Carefully position the first tile so that it is perfectly aligned with both chalk lines. Set the next few tiles along each axis. Then fill the area between the axes, working toward the walls. Set the tiles into place; don't slide them. Work very carefully. Minor errors can cause major alignment problems later on.

Continue laying tiles along each axis and filling in the area between them. If the room contains any obstructions, such as corners, pipes, or posts, cut tiles to fit around them. Make a template out of cardboard and trace its shape onto a tile. Use dividers to duplicate intricate shapes. Resilient tiles can be brittle when cold. They are easier to cut if they are first briefly warmed with a portable hair dryer or over a furnace.

Finishing Up

Finish the other three quadrants in the same manner as the first, starting in the center of the room and fanning out along both axes. To prevent displacement of newly laid tiles, lay a 2-foot by 2-foot piece of plywood over the tiles before walking or kneeling on them.

Be particularly careful about adhesive oozing out of the joints. Wipe it up immediately with a rag and a compatible solvent. Once adhesive sets it is very difficult to remove.

The Border

Sometimes tiles must be cut to fit against a wall. To do this mark each tile in its place. Set the tile to be cut directly on top of the last full tile in its row. Place a second tile on it and butt this second tile up against the wall so that part of it overlaps the first tile. Mark the first tile by scribing along the edge of the second tile with a pencil or a blade. Cut the first tile with a knife. Then apply adhesive and set it in place.

The Trim

Don't walk on the floor until the adhesive has set. Check the manufacturer's instructions for setup time. When the floor can safely be walked on, install the finish details. Vinyl cove base is usually the most attractive finish for resilient tile (see page 107). Install metal flat bars over transitions.

Measuring Border Tiles

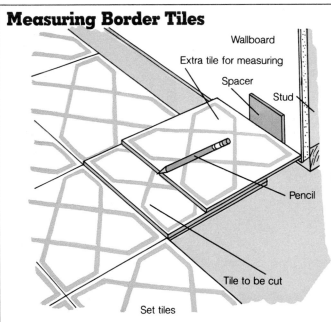

Wallboard

Extra tile for measuring

Spacer

Stud

Pencil

Tile to be cut

Set tiles

Installing the First Quadrant

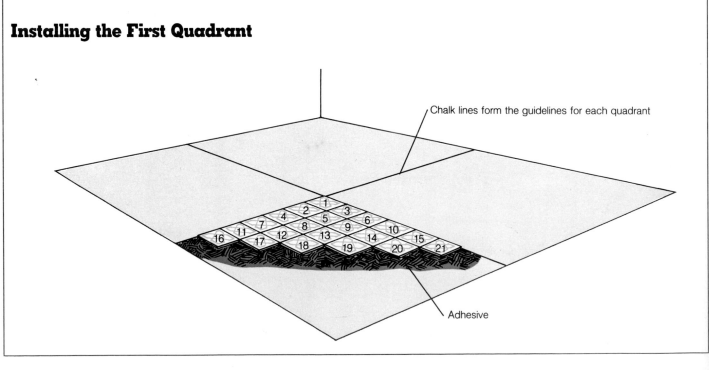

Chalk lines form the guidelines for each quadrant

Adhesive

Lightly mottled white resilient tiles have the look of marble in this elegant entryway. Setting the contrasting tiles diagonally adds to the visual width of the space, further increasing its grandness.

CERAMIC & DIMENSIONED STONE FLOORS

Ceramic tile is basically a slab of kiln-fired clay. This humble definition belies a product that is as good-looking as it is practical. Ceramic tile is tough, easy to clean, and fireproof. Tiles are also dazzlingly colorful and durable—some installations are older than written history.

Traditionally, tile was installed using a mortar bed, a tricky procedure. Although some installations are best left to professionals, most ceramic tile floors can be installed using the simple thinsetting techniques described in this chapter.

Improvements in the manufacturing of marble, slate, and granite tiles make them as easy to install as ceramic tile.

The issues of planning and design are relatively straightforward for ceramic and stone floors. The size of the tile and its shape, color, and texture work together with the grid and color of the grout lines to form an overall pattern.

Dimensioned stone tiles perform well both as a luxury tub surround and on the floor of this master bath. If installed properly these tiles hold up well against moisture.

CONSIDERING CERAMIC & DIMENSIONED STONE FLOORS

Both ceramic and dimensioned stone tile are easily installed by the do-it-yourselfer and require relatively little maintenance. Each type of tile adds special qualities to the character of the room because each is made from materials of the earth.

About Tiles

Ceramic tile is a manufactured product. Most ceramic tile is made from a combination of refined clay and ground shale or gypsum, plus talc, vermiculite, and sand. These elements are combined with water to form a mixture called bisque. Most commercial tile manufacturers use the extrusion method, in which green bisque is squeezed through a press into a die in the shape of the tile. The raw tiles are then fired in a kiln for anywhere from several hours to several days.

Unglazed tiles derive their color solely from the clay. Glazed tiles derive their color from their glaze—the transparent or colored coating on their top surface. Glazes are made up of lead silicates and pigments and are brushed or sprayed onto the surface of the bisque. Glaze can be applied to the raw bisque before it is fired, or it can be applied to fired tiles, which are then fired again. Glazes add color and protect the surface of the tile. Additives are sometimes mixed with the glaze to add texture as well.

In considering ceramic tile, be sure to choose a product that is designed for floors. Wall tiles are thinner than floor tiles and cannot withstand the pressure of a flooring installation.

Ceramic tiles are usually square; occasionally they are octagonal. They range in size from less than 2 inches to 18 inches square. The smallest tiles—called mosaics—are usually sold in sheets. Most floor tiles are 4 or 6 inches square.

Stone tiles are thin slices of solid marble, slate, granite, and other natural products cut to specific dimensions. They are a uniform, lightweight, and economical tile product that can be used in homes of every size and style. Most stone tiles are 12 inches square; a few are 6 inches by 12 inches.

Both ceramic and stone tiles tend to be cool to the touch—an advantage in hot weather but a possible source of discomfort in cold climates (unless it is installed over a radiant heating system or is used to collect solar heat). Tile is also heavier than most types of flooring; wood frame subfloors may have to be reinforced to carry the extra weight. The thicker materials will also raise the floor level; this may make them impractical where floor levels are established, where the raised level will interfere with cabinets and appliances, and where raised transitions to other rooms might be awkward.

Glazed ceramic tiles are water-resistant. The grout lines between them, however, are not—unless they are carefully sealed. Unglazed surfaces are water permeable, although they can be sealed against water absorption.

Tile tends to be slippery when wet; choose products with enough surface texture to provide adequate traction. Tile also tends to deflect sound rather than absorb it. If the acoustics of the room are important, use unglazed or textured materials, which absorb sound better than glazed tile, or consider using a different type of flooring.

Using Tile

Either ceramic or dimensioned stone tile can be used in any room in the house. Whether the entrance is a separate vestibule or merely part of the living room, it can be defined by the strong grid pattern of a tile installation. The total floor area of an entrance is usually small enough to make it possible to splurge on materials. Dimensioned stone tile makes a great first impression.

Tiles make a unique statement when used as accent pieces on stair risers.

Materials installed in kitchens must resist water, steam, grease, and odors. They must also be easy to clean. Ceramic tile fulfills all these requirements. Use tile on the floor and on the back splashes and countertops to create a coordinated design.

Surfaces in bathrooms have to withstand water, steam, moisture, and heat, and they too must be easy to clean. Tile is a perfect flooring material for bathrooms. Be sure to check the water absorbency of any tile destined to come in contact with water. When in doubt use a sealer. Around showers and tubs use glazed tiles with a matte finish or a texture for slip resistance. Tile can also be installed on tub and shower surrounds and on vanities for a well-coordinated bathroom.

Family room floors are another obvious choice for tile, which makes it easy to clean up messes caused by pets, children, and party guests. Floor tiles can also be installed around fireplaces and hearths to give a coordinated look to the family room as well.

The scale of the tile creates a visual effect that varies with the scale of the room. For example, in a large room small units tend to blend together to create an even pattern across the floor, large tiles will appear as distinct units. In a small room large tiles will jump out at the viewer, whereas smaller tiles will look quiet and appropriately in scale.

Because a tile floor is composed of many separate pieces, pattern tends to dominate the design. Tiles of contrasting colors can be used effectively to set a special pattern into the new floor, defining or separating spaces. This pattern may feature a wide border, a narrow band, or a geometric figure in the center of the room. Grout lines can also be part of the design. Grout in the same color as the tiles gives a clean-lined, tailored floor with a subdued grid. If a contrasting grout is used, the grid itself is highlighted and stands out.

Large, textured stone tiles help set the tone for this kitchen and pantry. Neither room is very large; the light-colored floor and the diagonal positioning of the tiles visually expand the space.

SELECTING CERAMIC & DIMENSIONED STONE MATERIALS

Installing a tile floor requires a considerable investment of time, money, and effort. However, due to the nature of the material, the floor isn't likely to be replaced for a long time. Be especially careful to select the right material for your floor.

Consider first where the material will be used. If water is likely to get on the floor, the surface finish and the width of the grout lines are important. Unglazed tile does not resist water or staining well enough for use in a kitchen unless it is sealed. Also, many kinds of tile are slippery when wet unless the surface is textured to provide traction.

The weight of tile—especially tile installed on a traditional mortar base—can overstress a wood frame floor and even the foundation below it, unless they are both designed to carry the load. Be sure to check this stress factor before deciding to use tile. This is very important if you are planning to install tile in a upper level of a multilevel house. Weight is not an issue when tile is installed on a concrete slab foundation. Today most tile is installed with thinset adhesive on a tile-backing unit laid over a rigid subfloor. This lightens the weight—compared to a mortar installation—but tile is still a heavy floor covering.

Surface finish, texture, and color each have a role to play. Dimpled or pocked tile looks hand wrought and casual. Smooth glazed tiles tend to look austere and refined. Color options range from vivid hues to neutral and natural tones. As with other materials, the more natural and neutral the color, the easier it will be to coordinate the floor with other elements in the overall design.

Tiles of two colors combine to form this large-scale grid, a beautiful master bedroom floor covering that provides the rich look of an ancient castle even in this modern home. This pattern can be replicated with less-expensive ceramic or resilient tile for a similar effect.

Ceramic and Dimensioned Stone Flooring Materials

	Ceramic Tile and Ceramic Mosaic	Unglazed Tile and Pavers	Dimensioned Stone Tile
Sizes and Shapes	1" to 6" ceramic mosaic, usually ¼" thick. 4" to 10" ceramic tile, from ⅜" to ½" thick. Squares, rectangles, and other geometric shapes. Rounded or squared edges.	4" to 12" units, ⅜" to ⅞" thick. Squares, rectangles, and random, roughly geometric shapes.	12" to 18" units, ¼" to ⅜" thick. Squares and rectangles.
Colors and Textures	Wide variety of brilliant and muted colors. Glossy, matte, or textured nonslip.	Natural earth tones, some blues and greens. Matte or textured nonslip.	Unusual colors and veining, depending on origin. Glossy or matte. Honed finish provides nonslip texture.
Finishes	Top layer is sealed when color glaze is baked on.	Unglazed tiles must be sealed to resist stains. They may be waxed.	Most should be sealed for best wear. Sealing darkens slate. Waxing is unnecessary.
Relative Cost	Medium to very high.	Medium to high.	Medium to very high.

Handmade paver tiles must be carefully installed and properly sealed for use in wet areas. The rich traditional look they provide is well worth the extra effort, however, as they will last for many years and can be adapted to a variety of kitchen styles.

PREPARING TO INSTALL CERAMIC TILE

Tile is a durable material that can last for centuries, but a tile floor is only as sound as the structure beneath it. Tile—including ceramic, marble, granite, slate, and pavers—is heavy. If the weight of the tile is greater than the subfloor and floor framing were designed to bear, it may be necessary to make structural changes before installing a tile floor.

A wood subfloor has a certain amount of give or springiness. This can cause a tile floor to crack at the grout lines or across individual tiles. To prevent this from happening, a double-wood subfloor (consisting of plywood nailed over the existing, well-fastened subfloor) is recommended when tile is installed over a wood frame substructure.

Because a concrete slab—particularly older concrete that has cured for some time—has no give, it makes an excellent base for setting tile flooring. Just be sure that there are no crumbly patches or areas where aggregate is exposed.

The chart on the opposite page summarizes the preparation steps for installing ceramic and dimensioned stone tile floors. It assumes that the existing floor is in good condition and that any moisture problems have been corrected. It tells what steps to take in most common situations. Consult the supplier, a licensed contractor, or the local building department for advice on how to deal with special conditions.

If the chart indicates that the existing flooring must be removed, refer to the chart after you have accomplished this step to see what needs to be done to prepare the surface that is now exposed.

Tools for Installing Ceramic Tile

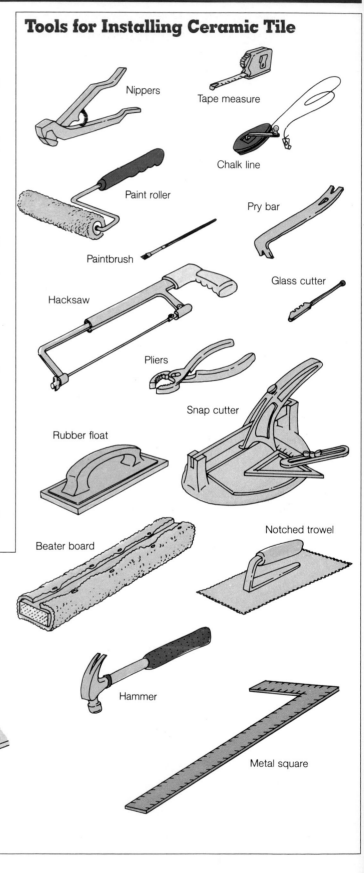

Nippers

Tape measure

Chalk line

Paint roller

Pry bar

Paintbrush

Glass cutter

Hacksaw

Pliers

Snap cutter

Rubber float

Beater board

Notched trowel

Hammer

Metal square

Making a Jury Stick

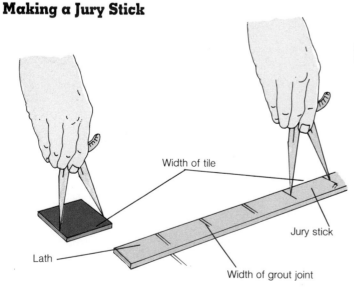

Width of tile

Jury stick

Lath

Width of grout joint

Preparation Steps for Ceramic Tile Installations

This chart summarizes the preparation steps required for installing ceramic tile materials over various existing floors.

Existing Floor	Preparation for Ceramic Tile
Exposed Joists	• Install a double-wood subfloor. First, install ¾" T&G CDX plywood directly over the joists. Then install underlayment-grade plywood or tile-backing units over the subfloor.
Bare Concrete	• Make surface repairs to slab as needed. • Roughen the surface for best adhesion.
Wood Subfloor	
Over Wood Frame	• Make surface repairs as needed. • Install underlayment-grade plywood. • Install tile-backing units over subfloor.
Over Concrete Slab	• Remove all wood materials to expose the slab. • Make surface repairs to slab as needed. • Roughen the surface for best adhesion.
Wood Finish Floor	
Over Wood Frame	• Remove finish flooring to expose the subfloor. • Install underlayment-grade plywood.
Over Concrete Slab	• Remove all wood materials to expose the slab. • Make surface repairs to slab as needed. • Roughen the surface for best adhesion.
Resilient Sheet or Tile	
Over Wood Frame	• Do not remove or sand older resilient flooring that may contain asbestos fibers. If in doubt about the flooring you wish to cover, seek professional help. • If the resilient flooring is installed over particleboard underlayment, remove both. • If the resilient flooring is installed over plywood, is dense (neither cushioned nor springy), and is sound, remove wax or finish. Otherwise remove the flooring to expose the subfloor. • Install underlayment-grade plywood or tile-backing units over the subfloor.
Over Concrete Slab	• Do not remove or sand older resilient flooring that may contain asbestos fibers. If in doubt about the flooring you wish to cover, seek professional help. • If the resilient flooring is cushioned, springy, or unsound, remove it and make surface repairs to slab as needed. • Otherwise remove wax or finish and select an adhesive that is compatible with the resilient flooring.
Ceramic Tile	
Over Wood Frame	• If possible, remove existing tile. Otherwise secure loose tiles and roughen the surface for best adhesion. If surface is uneven, smooth it with a liquid underlayment. New tile can be glued down directly with appropriate adhesive. • If existing tile can be removed, install underlayment-grade plywood or tile-backing units over the subfloor.
Over Concrete Slab	• If possible, remove existing tile. Otherwise secure loose tiles and roughen the surface for best adhesion. If surface is uneven, smooth it with a liquid underlayment. New tile can be glued down directly with appropriate adhesive. • If existing tile can be removed, make surface repairs to slab as needed.
Carpet	
Over Wood Frame	• Remove existing carpet and pad. • Install underlayment-grade plywood or tile-backing units over the subfloor.
Over Concrete Slab	• Remove existing carpet and pad. • Make surface repairs to slab as needed.

INSTALLING CERAMIC TILE

Setting ceramic tile is a good do-it-yourself project because the professional labor costs are high but most of the work is repetitive and is easy to master with a little practice. Tile-setting tools can usually be rented from ceramic-tile dealers.

To Begin

The procedures illustrated and described on these pages are appropriate for uniformly colored tile floors in rooms that pose no special problems.

Stone tiles are slightly more difficult to install than ceramic tiles. They must be cut with a power tile-cutting saw, which can be rented from most tile dealers. The joints must be tighter than generally used for ceramic tile, allowing for less flexiblity in layout. The natural graining of the stones may pose some placement questions. If the installation is straightforward and plenty of time is allowed for the design phase, a handy do-it-yourselfer should have no problem designing and installing a stone floor.

Install all tiles over a smooth, sound, rigid, and properly prepared subfloor (see page 18). The instructions in this section describe the thinset method of installation. Tile-backing units make the best base for all tile installations. Remember that tile-backing units are not structurally sound. They must be installed over a plywood subfloor.

Make sure that all doors will clear the new floor (see page 22). Tile can be set to the existing baseboards. However, tile base borders are very effective with a ceramic tile floor. If you plan to remove the existing trim, do so before beginning the layout. If you do not remove it, protect it from splashes of adhesive and grout.

Layout

Begin the installation along the most visually prominent axis and proceed toward an exit, to avoid walking on freshly laid tiles. Since the wall may not be straight or may be out of square with the sidewalls, snap chalk lines to work from. Then measure out from the starting wall, at both ends, a distance equal to one tile width plus two grout lines. Make marks to indicate this distance and snap a chalk line between them.

Repeat this procedure for the other three walls, squaring each line to the previous one by holding a framing square at each corner or using a 3-4-5 triangle (see page 32). When all four lines are laid out, double-check for square by measuring both diagonals. You now have perimeter guidelines that will ensure a straight row of tiles against the starting wall and will keep the starting end of each new row squared to the previous rows.

Adhesives and Mortars for Tile Floors

This chart offers an overview of the different types of adhesive and mortar that are used for ceramic and dimensioned stone tile installations. Use it along with the manufacturer's specifications to help you to select the right adhesive. Consult with the tile dealer about the specific conditions of your installation.

Adhesives and Mortars	Composition	Conditions for Use	Comments
Type I Mastic	Organic based	For damp areas.	Ready to use. Flammable; may irritate skin and lungs.
Type II Mastic	Latex based	For dry areas only.	Easy to clean up. Nonflammable.
Dry-Set Mortar	Portland cement mixed with sand, additives, and water	For concrete or tile-backing units. Not recommended for use over wood or resilient floors.	Not water-resistant. Easy to clean up; rigid; impact resistant. Nonflammable.
Latex-Portland Cement Mortar	Portland cement mixed with sand and liquid latex, sometimes diluted with water	For concrete or tile-backing units. Not recommended for use over wood or resilient floors.	More water-resistant than dry-set mortar. Easier to work with; less rigid; tends to move.
Epoxy Adhesive	Epoxy resin mixed with hardener	Preferred adhesive for moisture-prone areas. Use over plywood, tile-backing units, or existing resilient floors.	Expensive. Works best between 70° and 85° F. Toxic to skin.
Epoxy Mortar	Epoxy resin mixed with hardener, sand, and portland cement	Preferred adhesive for moisture-prone areas. Use over concrete, tile-backing units, or existing ceramic tile.	More body and more chemical resistance than adhesive. Levels uneven subsurfaces.

Next, test the layout. Lay rows of loose tiles along each perimeter guideline from wall to wall. Set plastic spacers between them for the grout lines. These are sold at tile stores in a range of sizes. Choose spacers that equal the width of the grout lines that you allowed for when you snapped the chalk lines. Some tiles have lugs molded into their edges that serve as spacers. This test run will indicate whether it will be necessary to cut tiles at the walls. If cut tiles must be used, decide where to use them. It may be possible to avoid cuts at one or all of the walls simply by altering the width of the grout spaces. If the grout width is altered in one direction, however, it must be altered in the other direction as well. Experiment with the test run to find the layout that will be the most pleasing to look at and that will require the fewest cuts.

Make a jury stick to ensure perfect tile placement (see page 82). A jury stick is a homemade measuring device created for a particular tile installation. Units of measure indicate the width of the tiles and the grout joints between them. Make a jury stick out of a straight piece of lattice, 1 by 3, or similar lumber about 8 to 10 feet long. Mark off equal segments that represent the width of one tile plus one grout width.

Measure and mark the exact tile and grout widths along the length of 1 by 3 material. Hold the jury stick against the chalk lines to align the tiles as you set them out into the field.

Slate, as used on this kitchen floor, is one of several natural products that are classified as dimensioned stone tile. Be sure to check each tile prior to installation. The coloring and veining varies greatly from tile to tile; use this variety to enhance, rather than to distract from, the pattern that you've developed.

Setting the First Tiles

Use a notched trowel to apply the adhesive. Spread it with the smooth side of the trowel and comb it into ridges with the notched side. Use the size of notched trowel recommended on the package. Spread no more than 1 square yard of adhesive at first, until you see how quickly it sets up. Spread it right up to the perimeter guidelines, but do not cover them. Wear gloves if you are working with epoxy.

Set the first tile at the corner where the chalk lines abut. Place the tile down onto the adhesive with a gentle twisting motion, but do not slide it into place. Check the alignment using the jury stick. Complete the starter row, placing plastic spacers between the tiles as you go. These can be left in place until the joints are grouted. Immediately clean off any adhesive that oozes onto the surface of the tile, using an appropriate solvent. Remove excess adhesive between tiles with a cotton swab or a thin stick.

When you have covered all of the first adhesive, "beat" the tiles in with a beater board. This is a handmade carpet-covered board used with a hammer to force the tiles into the adhesive and to level them. Check the surface of the new floor with a level to make sure that it is even.

Cutting Tiles

It may be necessary to cut tiles at the end of the row. The illustration shows how to mark border tiles for cutting. If the layout is regular and perfectly square and the tile spacing is consistent, cut several tiles ahead of time. Postpone any irregular cuts until the full row of tiles is set. Often the tile dealer will make the cuts for you. Otherwise rent a snap cutter for easy cuts and a tile-cutting saw for difficult cuts, multiple cuts, or any cuts on dimensioned stone tiles. Follow instructions and wear appropriate safety equipment when operating a tile-cutting saw.

In tiling around pipes or fixtures, such as a toilet, it may be necessary to make small cuts in several tiles to form a curved line. Use tile nippers, available where tiles are sold.

Setting the Field

Start the second and all succeeding rows of the tile field at the same end as the first. Butt each starter tile against the layout stick and each succeeding tile in the new row against the installed row adjacent to it. Use plastic spacers wherever tiles meet. Check placements regularly with your jury stick.

Set cut tiles, border tiles, and other tiles in tight places using the back-butter method. Apply a small amount of adhesive on the back of the tile and comb it with the notched side of the trowel. Make sure that the adhesive covers the entire back of the tile. Set the tile in place, using a slight twisting motion. Level it with the beater board.

Before kneeling or walking on set tile, lay down a small piece of plywood to distribute your body weight more evenly across the surface. Finish the installation by setting the remaining border tiles. Start at the original corner and guide

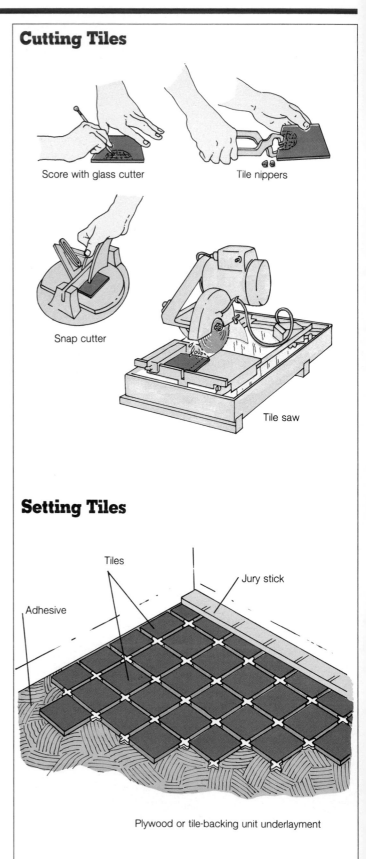

Cutting Tiles

Score with glass cutter

Tile nippers

Snap cutter

Tile saw

Setting Tiles

Tiles

Jury stick

Adhesive

Plywood or tile-backing unit underlayment

Leveling Tiles

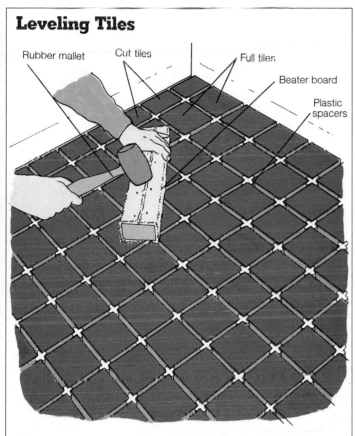

Rubber mallet
Cut tiles
Full tiles
Beater board
Plastic spacers

Grouting and Finishing the Joints

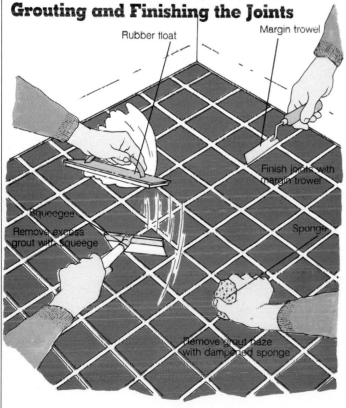

Rubber float
Margin trowel
Finish joints with margin trowel
Squeegee
Remove excess grout with squeegee
Sponge
Remove grout haze with dampened sponge

their placement from the existing installation, not from the walls. Beat them into place and clean off any adhesive or dust.

The instructions on the package will specify how long the adhesive must cure prior to grouting. Avoid walking on tiles that are setting up because the tiles may become dislodged. Also, the edges are brittle and easily chipped.

Grouting

Before grouting remove the spacers from the joints. Some grout is premixed. If you will be mixing it, prepare just enough for the amount of grouting you will do at one time. Do not attempt to remoisten dried grout. Mix the grout to a mayonnaiselike consistency, following the manufacturer's instructions.

Dump a batch of grout onto the surface of the tile and spread it into the joints with a rubber float, obtainable from tile stores. Be sure that the joints are tightly filled, with no voids or air pockets. If necessary, use the handle of an old toothbrush or some similar object to pack the grout into the joints. Work the float diagonally across the field in both directions to scrape away excess grout. Avoid wiping parallel to the grout joints.

After 10 to 15 minutes, use a moist rounded-edged sponge to remove as much grout residue as possible. Rinse the sponge and wring it out frequently. Allow the grout to set up for about 30 minutes.

A film of dry grout will appear on the surface of the tiles. Wipe it off with a nearly dry sponge, terry-cloth rag, or cheesecloth. This process also polishes the tiles. Use the toothbrush handle to tool and finish any joints that are not smooth. Be sure to remove all the grout haze now. It is extremely difficult to remove after it has cured.

Allow the grout to cure according to the manufacturer's instructions. For best results cover the freshly grouted installation with plastic sheeting for the first 24 hours. This will keep it from drying too fast, which can cause it to crack.

Sealing

Some types of tile, some grout, and some locations require a final coat of sealer. Apply it two or three weeks after grouting, following the manufacturer's directions. To seal the tiles use a large brush or a paint roller. If only the grout is being sealed, apply the sealer carefully with a small brush. Immediately wipe any sealer off tiles with a damp cloth.

Finishing Up

To install tile base borders, attach them to the wall with adhesive at the same time as you lay the floor. Place joint spacers or shims between the floor tiles and the wall tiles and between all the wall tiles. Grout and seal them at the same time, using the same techniques as you used on the floor. See page 107 for more information on installing tile base borders.

Install wood baseboards or vinyl cove after the tile is installed, grouted, and sealed (see page 106). If the tiles are all level the trim should snug tightly to the floor and leave no unsightly gaps. Rehang the doors.

CARPET FLOORS

With its wide range of colors, fibers, and textures, carpet is one of the most luxurious choices for flooring. Its softness and resilience invite you to sit down or stretch out on the floor itself. The higher and denser the pile and the thicker the pad, the warmer and quieter it is to walk on. A broad expanse of carpet creates a simple sweep of color that serves as a quiet visual foundation for the room and, at the same time, greets the eye with a delicate play of light and luster. Because carpet is thick and flexible and is usually laid over a pad, it can be used on floors that have surface irregularities. When other flooring choices might require extensive preparation of the subfloor, carpeting may provide an effective way to transform the room easily and quickly.

Whatever the floor covering, the installation project is finished only when the trim has been replaced and the doors have been rehung. These tasks are discussed in this chapter as well. When complete, move the furniture back in and enjoy your new floor.

Three colors of carpet combine for spectacular effect in this living room. Careful planning, measuring, and cutting produce an installed carpet featuring all the tones in the interior design. Extra carpet was used to make the entrance area rug. Carpeted stairs mute noise and soften the expanse.

CONSIDERING CARPET

The variety of carpets can seem bewildering at first, as can the claims that each manufacturer makes for its own product. Obtain as much information as possible and compare claims and prices before you buy. Ask friends whether they are pleased with their carpet. Is it wearing well? Is it easy to clean?

When considering carpet, keep in mind the nature of the material as it relates to the function of the room. For example, is the floor likely to get wet? Because many pads, carpet backings, and pile fibers are absorbent, a carpeted floor can be subject to moisture damage. For installation in kitchens and bathrooms, choose fibers that resist moisture and mildew. If ventilation is a problem, consider some other kind of flooring.

Because carpet is thick and flexible and is usually laid over a pad, it can be used on floors that have surface irregularities. When other flooring choices might require extensive preparation of the subfloor, carpeting may provide an effective way to transform the room easily and quickly.

Be completely practical when choosing carpet. Think of the worst-case scenario—puppy puddles, young children's muddy shoes, sparks from the fireplace, a spilled glass of cranberry juice—and plan accordingly. Pattern can help to disguise stains.

Be very picky about finishing and about all the details of installation. If the carpet is properly installed, it will look handsome and stay in fine condition for many years.

Carpet for heavy-traffic rooms, such as kitchens and entrances, must be carefully chosen. A hard, high-density carpet with a small pattern is a good choice; it provides insurance against the inevitable stains, marks, and scuffs. Look for carpet that is specifically designed for high-volume use.

Using carpet on stairways and hallways solves noise problems, softens the wide expanse, and forms a visual link between areas and levels within a house. However, the high traffic on stairways and hallways produces a lot of wear-and-tear, often causing this carpet to wear out sooner than the carpet in adjoining rooms. There are several carpet alternatives to help solve this problem.

Consider using high-density carpet on hallways and stairways. In order to retain the visual benefits of matching different carpets within the house, purchase high-density carpet in the same color as the carpet used in other areas of the house. Or use the high-density carpet in the center and the plush carpet on the edges. This technique for a stairway is shown in the photograph on page 37.

If using two different carpets is not feasible, consider purchasing extra carpet, keeping it well stored, and replacing the hallway and stairway carpets about halfway through the lifetime of the rest of the carpet in the house.

Another alternative for stairways is to install carpet along the center—for a runner effect—and finish the edges with wood or tile. This is especially effective for a main stairway—the runner effect makes any stairway look quite grand.

A luxurious carpet adds warmth and comfort to the living room and makes it look more welcoming to guests. It sets the stage beautifully for favorite furniture and brings together the design of the room. In family rooms choose a practical carpet that resists stains and spills but one that is soft enough to sit or lie on.

A single sweep of soft, comfortable carpet makes the bedroom an inviting place. It adds warmth on cold mornings, encouraging the most reluctant riser to get up. Carpet cuts down on noise, converting the bedroom into a restful retreat. Choose the most practical carpet for children's rooms.

Carpet can make a cool bathroom cozy. It takes the cold edge off slick-surfaced fixtures and provides a touch of comfort and luxury. Look for moisture-resistant fibers, mildewproof pads, and easy-to-clean weaves. Consider too installing tile around the shower, washbasin, and tub and reserving the carpet for the drier parts of the bathroom.

Carpet gives the room a broad, expansive, soft look and comes in a wide range of colors

and textures. Both of these features speak with a potentially strong voice. If bold color is important, choose an even texture. If the carpet has a lot of texture, choose a quiet color.

Bright, vivid colors are enticing on the swatch, but be careful! In large amounts they can be overwhelming and they can lose their appeal over time. Neutral colors, such as beige, taupe, cream, celadon, and gray are generally a good choice. They provide a versatile background that does not conflict with the overall interior design scheme and they are adaptable to changes in room decoration.

To ensure that the carpet installation is both cost-effective and enduringly attractive, plan the layout carefully. Pay attention to the carpet pile and the seams.

Carpet pile—whether it is looped, cut, or sculptured—has a definite direction, or nap. To get the most lustrous visual effect of color and texture as you enter the room, install carpet with the pile leaning toward the doorway.

If it will be necessary to seam the carpet, make sure that the pile of each piece runs in the same direction, so that the visual effect is one of a continuous surface. This will also help to conceal the seams. Avoid placing seams in heavy-traffic areas, and never place one across a doorway; traffic will eventually take its toll and loosen the stitches. Whenever possible keep seams perpendicular to the largest window openings, so that they run parallel to the rays of light; this will make them less visible.

Using the same floor covering in several areas will link the spaces together and suggest an expansive quality. The use of the same plush carpet in several rooms and hallways, as shown here, makes a small house seem larger.

SELECTING CARPET MATERIALS

Some fibers age better than others. This can affect the quality of the carpet. The best carpets are made of wool. However, manufacturers have been steadily improving the quality of artificial fibers over the last 40 years. Today there are many beautiful and durable synthetics available that are less expensive than wool.

The characteristics of individual fibers and the way in which the fibers are joined both affect carpet durability.

Weave is the first important consideration. Ninety-eight percent of all carpet sold is tufted—the yarn is pushed through a primary backing to form loops and then is bonded to a secondary backing. In the remaining 2 percent, the yarn itself is woven together like a tapestry to form its own backing. Woven carpet is more expensive than tufted carpet.

Consider density as well. Carpet manufacturers list density as the number of yarns per square inch. Generally the more yarn per square inch, the more durable the carpet.

Each piece of yarn in a carpet twists out from the backing. This twist gives the carpet resilience; when crushed it springs back readily into shape. The greater the twist, the higher the quality of the carpet.

Quality is almost always directly related to cost—you get what you pay for. But shop around. Count in the price of the pad when comparing the cost of carpet to that of other types of flooring, and don't forget the installation fees. Store sales quite often include discounts on pads and installation. In general, carpet costs have not risen as rapidly as the costs of other types of flooring.

Opposite: A tight-weave carpet presents a tailored look for this contemporary bedroom. Tight-weave carpets show fewer footprints than do plush carpets and, therefore, are good choices for heavy-traffic areas.

Carpet Flooring Materials

	Wool	Nylon	Polyester	Acrylic	Polypropylene Olefin
Resiliency	Excellent. Feels springy underfoot.	Very good. Resists crushing.	Fair. May crush.	Good. Almost as resilient as wool.	Differs depending on construction and type of pile.
Resistance to:					
Soil	Very good. When soiled may be difficult to clean.	Very good. More easily cleaned than wool.	Fair. Cleans well.	Good. Must be treated after deep cleaning.	Very good. Doesn't hold soil.
Abrasion	Very good.	Very good.	Excellent.	Poor.	Very good.
Static	Tends to hold static unless treated.	Metal threads almost always included to resist static.	Not prone to static.	Will not hold static.	Will not hold static.
Fading	Damaged by direct sunlight over time.	Damaged by direct sunlight over time.	Damaged by heat and sunlight.	High color life.	Usually treated to resist fading.
Mildew and Pests	Usually treated to resist damage from mildew and pests.	Fiber naturally resists damage from mildew and pests.	Usually treated to resist damage from mildew. Not likely to attract pests.	Fiber naturally resists damage from mildew and pests.	Fiber naturally resists damage from mildew and pests.
Relative Cost	High.	Medium to high.	Low to medium.	Low to medium.	Low.

PREPARING TO INSTALL CARPET

Except for cushion-backed or very thin goods, carpet conceals defects in the subsurface quite well; the thicker the pad or carpet, the better.

To Begin

In general, carpet installations require very little preparation. The subfloor must be dry, free of debris, and essentially smooth. If an existing carpet is being replaced, it is possible to reuse the old pad and tackless strip, provided that they are in good condition. However, pad is not that expensive. Be sure that it is clean and free of odors and mildew before reusing.

Concrete slab subfloors with radiant-heat pipes pose a special problem: If you nail down tackless strip (see page 96), you risk puncturing a pipe. To locate the pipes moisten the slab around the perimeter of the room wherever the tackless strip is to be nailed down. Then turn up the heat. Mark with chalk the areas that dry first. These are the spots to avoid when nailing.

If there are unique conditions or you are unsure of the pipe location, consult the supplier, a professional carpet installer, or the local building department for assistance.

If the chart indicates that the existing flooring must be removed, refer to the chart after you have accomplished this step to see what needs to be done to prepare the flooring surface that is now exposed.

Storing and Handling

Store carpet on a clean surface in a dry area. If the surface is damp, lay a sheet of plastic underneath the carpet roll. To

rough-cut the material to size, cut pieces off the roll in a large, clean, dry, open area, such as a spacious room or even the driveway or the basement. Then carry the pieces separately into the rooms where they will be installed. In general, roll and unroll carpet in the direction of the pile.

Its weight and bulk make carpet awkward to handle; you may need a helper. One good way to handle a large unrolled piece of carpet for carrying is to fold both long sides toward the center and then loosely roll it up. The shorter roll is bulky but easier to maneuver.

Tools for Installing Carpet

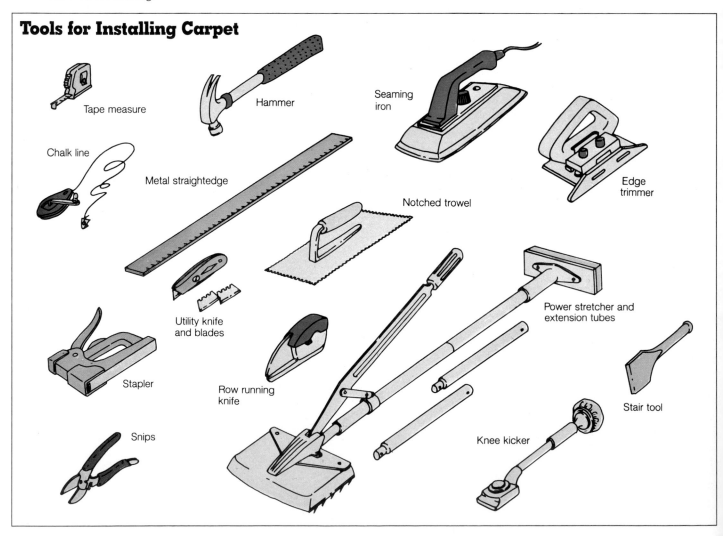

Tape measure

Chalk line

Hammer

Seaming iron

Metal straightedge

Notched trowel

Edge trimmer

Utility knife and blades

Stapler

Row running knife

Power stretcher and extension tubes

Stair tool

Knee kicker

Snips

Preparation Steps for Carpet Installations

This chart summarizes the preparation steps required for installing carpet over various existing floors and floor systems.

Existing Floor	Preparation for Conventional Carpet	Preparation for Cushion-Backed Carpet
Exposed Joists	• Install ¾" T&G CDX plywood subfloor. • If carpet is thin, fill joints and surface depressions and sand smooth, or use CDX/PTS plywood.	• Install ¾" T&G CDX/PTS plywood subfloor. • Fill joints and surface depressions and sand smooth.
Bare Concrete	• Make surface repairs to slab as needed.	• Make surface repairs to slab as needed.
Wood Subfloor		
Over Wood Frame	• Make surface repairs as needed. • If subfloor is very rough or uneven or has gaps between boards, install ⅜"–½" underlayment-grade plywood.	• Make surface repairs as needed. • If subfloor is very rough or uneven or has gaps between the boards, install ⅜"–½" underlayment-grade plywood. • Fill joints and surface depressions and sand smooth.
Over Concrete Slab	• Remove all wood materials to expose the slab. • Make surface repairs to slab as needed.	• Remove all wood materials to expose the slab. • Make surface repairs to slab as needed.
Wood Finish Floor		
Over Wood Frame	• Make surface repairs to existing floor as needed.	• Make surface repairs to existing floor as needed. • Install ⅜"–½" underlayment-grade plywood. • Fill joints and surface depressions and sand smooth.
Over Concrete Slab	• Remove all wood materials to expose the slab. • Make surface repairs to slab as needed.	• Remove all wood materials to expose the slab. • Make surface repairs to slab as needed.
Resilient Sheet or Tile		
Over Wood Frame	• Do not remove or sand older resilient flooring that may contain asbestos fibers. If in doubt about the flooring you wish to cover, seek professional help. • Make surface repairs to existing floor as needed.	• If resilient flooring is smooth and tightly bonded, remove wax and roughen surface for best adhesion. • If resilient flooring is not well bonded, remove it. Install ⅜"–½" underlayment-grade plywood. Fill joints and surface depressions and sand smooth.
Over Concrete Slab	• Make surface repairs to existing floor as needed.	• If resilient flooring is smooth and tightly bonded, make surface repairs as needed. Remove wax and roughen surface for best adhesion. • If resilient flooring is not well bonded, remove it. Install ⅜"–½" underlayment-grade plywood. Fill joints and surface depressions and sand smooth.
Ceramic Tile		
Over Wood Frame	• If possible, remove existing tile. Otherwise make surface repairs as needed. Smooth and even out the surface with a liquid underlayment.	• If possible, remove existing tile. • Otherwise make surface repairs as needed. Smooth and even out the surface with a liquid underlayment compatible with the carpet adhesive.
Over Concrete Slab	• If tile is smooth and tightly bonded, even out the surface with a liquid underlayment. • Otherwise remove it and make surface repairs to slab as needed.	• If possible, remove existing tile and make surface repairs to slab as needed. • Otherwise smooth and even out the surface with a liquid underlayment compatible with the carpet adhesive.
Carpet		
Over Wood Frame	• Remove existing carpet and pad. Make surface repairs to subfloor as needed. • If subfloor is very rough or uneven or has gaps between boards, install ⅜"–½" underlayment-grade plywood.	• Remove existing carpet and pad. • Make surface repairs to subfloor as needed. • If subfloor is very rough or uneven or has gaps between boards, install ⅜"–½" underlayment-grade plywood. Fill joints and surface depressions and sand smooth.
Over Concrete Slab	• Remove existing carpet and pad. • Make surface repairs to slab as needed.	• Remove existing carpet and pad. • Make surface repairs to slab as needed.

INSTALLING CONVENTIONAL CARPET

A proper installation is vital to getting good wear from the carpet. It requires at least basic carpentry skills to install the tackless strip. Installing the carpet itself takes these skills and also physical strength. You must be able to measure accurately, lift entire rolls of carpet and padding, and pull and stretch with force.

To Begin

For most carpet installations it is unneccessary to remove the baseboards, although you may have to touch them up with paint or finish later. Test to see whether the new carpet and pad will block the doors. If they will, measure, mark, remove, and trim the doors before beginning the installation.

Doorways

If the subfloor is concrete, nail a special gripper edge across the doorway using concrete nails to fasten it down. The teeth bite the carpet, and the curved metal flange is hammered down over the edge to bind the carpet's edge.

If the subfloor is a nailable surface, this type of metal strip makes a clean binding where the carpet butts an adjacent floor surface. This type of binding is visible.

If you do not want a visible strip to bind the edge, and if your installation will accommodate this type of binding, consider using a special Z-bar. Nail it under a length of tackless strip installed in the door opening. The carpet wraps over the Z and is clinched by it.

The Tackless Strip

Use the type of strip specified for the carpet backing. If the strip will be anchored to a wood surface, use tackless strip with wood nails; use tackless strip with masonry nails on concrete.

If the tackless strip is to be nailed to concrete, make sure that the concrete will hold the nails. Drive a few nails into the slab around the edge. If they don't hold well, the strip should be glued down with a special adhesive. Whether the strip is nailed or glued to a concrete floor, there may be places where you suspect that it will not hold. Use a double row of strip in those areas.

Nails driven into concrete covered with resilient flooring may not hold well. The thickness of the flooring will reduce their penetration and their bite. Try longer nails or scrape away a 2-inch margin of resilient flooring all around the room and install a thicker tackless strip directly on the concrete.

To lay carpet over ceramic tile, rough up the glazed surface with sandpaper where the tackless strip will be installed. This will break the sheen and make a better bond. Then glue down the tackless strip.

Starting in one corner nail strip around the perimeter of the room. The pins should point toward the wall. Leave a gap between strip and wall equal to two thirds of the thickness of the carpet. Cut pieces to length. Each piece should be held in place by at least two nails. Have extra nails on hand to fasten short lengths of strip. Follow all the angles, such as those around door casings or trim, and fit the pieces around the perimeter of the room.

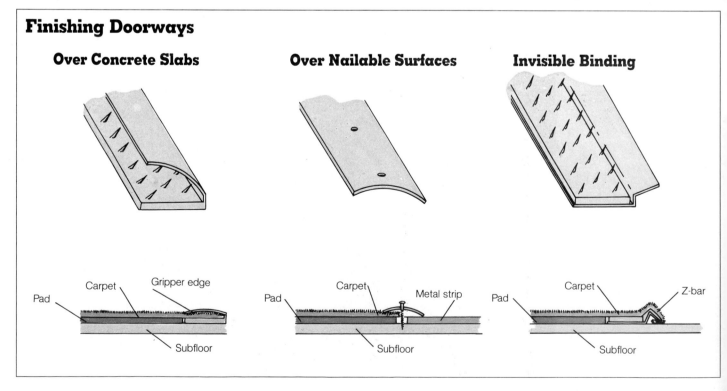

Finishing Doorways

Over Concrete Slabs
Over Nailable Surfaces
Invisible Binding

The dark background of this patterned carpet gives substance to the high-ceiling room, and the contrasting tan keeps the floor covering from overpowering the room. Experiment with various patterns before choosing your carpet.

Installing Carpet Pad

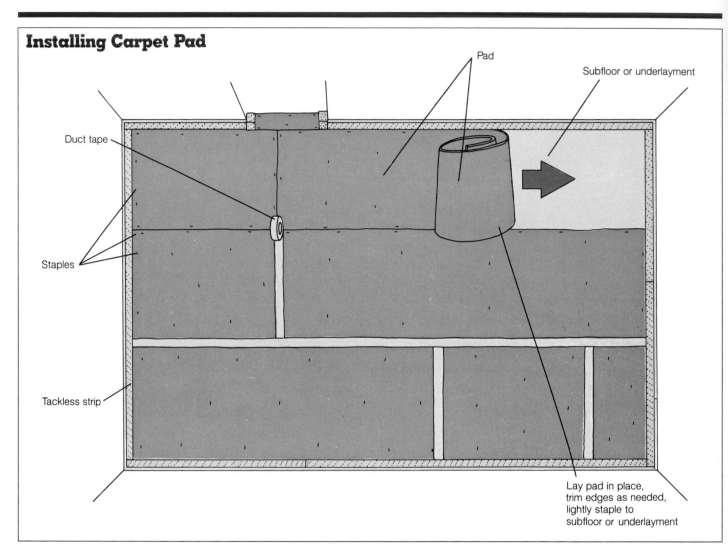

Pad

Subfloor or underlayment

Duct tape

Staples

Tackless strip

Lay pad in place,
trim edges as needed,
lightly staple to
subfloor or underlayment

The Pad

Using a utility knife, cut a piece from the roll of pad long enough to cover one end of the room. Position the piece just short of the tackless strip along its long edge. It should overlap the strip at both of its ends. Use a staple hammer to fasten it down every 6 to 12 inches all the way around. Staples should hold the pad firmly to the subfloor, but be sure that the tops of the staples do not perforate the pad. If the pad is waffled, staple into the depressions. Pull out any loose staples; they can work up through the carpet later. To install a pad on a concrete floor, fasten special paper tape around the edge of the pad so that it laps onto the pins of the tackless strip.

Continue cutting and fastening the pad until the entire floor is covered. Butt the edges; don't overlap them. To trim the perimeter of the pad, run a utility knife along the edge of the tackless strip, holding it at a slight angle to bevel the edge of the pad toward the strip. Increase the angle for a foam pad. This leaves sufficient space at the edge so that the pad won't ride up onto the tackless strip when the carpet is installed.

The Carpet

Find an area where the carpet can be laid out flat. Be sure that this area is clean and dry. If necessary, lay down a sheet of plastic to protect the carpet.

Before measuring the first cut, square the end of the carpet by folding it back 3 or 4 feet so that the side edges line up over each other. Measure the distance from the front corner back to the fold at both sides. These distances will be equal if the end is cut square to the side edges. If the measurements are not equal, square the carpet by measuring along the longer edge, starting at the fold, a distance equal to the shorter edge. Make a mark and then take all measurements along that edge from the mark rather than from the corner. Notch the mark so that it will be visible from both sides of the carpet. When you make the measurements, leave wall and seam allowances of 2 or 3 inches; these will be trimmed to fit later.

If the carpet has loop pile in straight rows, cut it from the face side, using a row cutter or a utility knife. Before making the cut use a screwdriver to clear the cutting path by separating the rows of pile.

Cut other carpets from the back. First, working from the face side, measure the carpet along both edges. Mark the points from which you will cut with a small notch or slit. Roll back the carpet far enough to snap a chalk line across the back side between the two notches. Using a straightedge, cut with a utility knife just deep enough to sever the backing. Separate the pieces carefully, cutting any pile yarn that holds them together.

Unroll each piece so that the pile runs in the correct direction, with the first edge lapping slightly up the wall. At corners and obstructions make relief cuts by slitting vertically through the 2- to 3-inch seam allowance, just deep enough to let the carpet lie flat.

Overlap pieces by 1 inch or so. Check to see that the pile of both pieces runs in the same direction.

Cut the seam edges on both pieces perfectly straight and parallel. For a loop pile carpet, position the pieces so that the edges are parallel, with the pile of both pieces running in the same direction and the edges overlapping at least 1 inch.

Using the edge of the top piece as a guide, cut the bottom piece with a row cutter. Finish the cut with a utility knife at the edges where the carpet laps up the wall.

Note: If the seam is in a doorway or other location where exact placement is necessary, stretch the first piece of carpet into place before trimming and seaming.

Installing Carpet

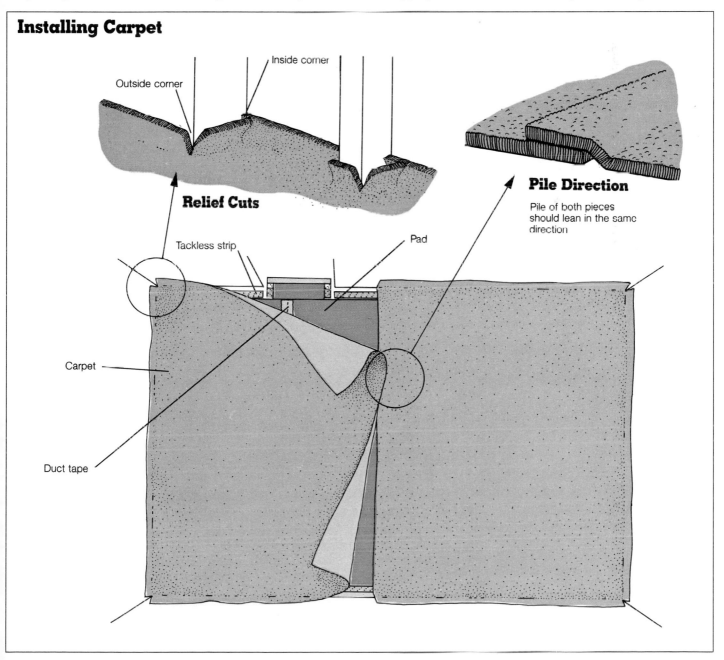

Outside corner

Inside corner

Relief Cuts

Pile Direction

Pile of both pieces should lean in the same direction

Tackless strip

Pad

Carpet

Duct tape

Seaming Carpet

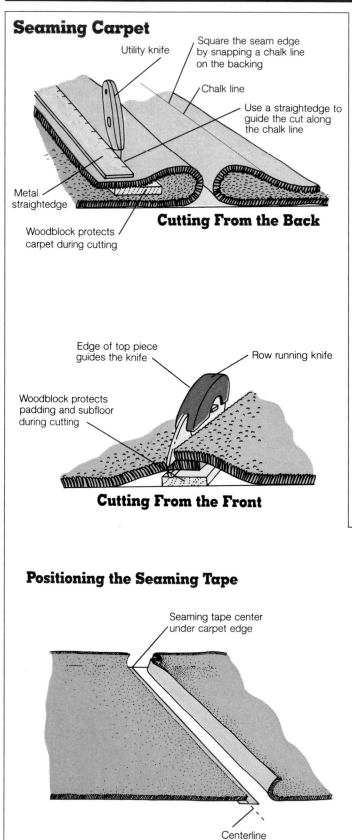

Cutting From the Back

- Utility knife
- Square the seam edge by snapping a chalk line on the backing
- Chalk line
- Use a straightedge to guide the cut along the chalk line
- Metal straightedge
- Woodblock protects carpet during cutting

Cutting From the Front

- Edge of top piece guides the knife
- Row running knife
- Woodblock protects padding and subfloor during cutting

Positioning the Seaming Tape

- Seaming tape center under carpet edge
- Centerline

Seaming

Cut a length of hot-melt seaming tape to the exact length of the seam. Center it under the seam with the adhesive side up, lifting one of the carpet edges and sliding the tape into place. Heat the tape with a special seaming iron or an old clothes iron warmed to 250° F. Slip the iron onto the tape at one end of the seam and let both pieces of carpet flop onto the top of the iron. Glide the iron slowly along the tape, about 1 foot every 30 seconds, pressing the carpet edges tightly together along each just-heated section. Move the iron with one hand while holding the edges together with the other. Keep the pile out of the adhesive and check to make sure that the backings butt tightly together. As you move away from each heated section, place some books or other flat heavy objects on it to hold the seam together.

Continue seaming until you get as close as possible to the far wall. Let the seamed carpet set and cool for 5 or 10 minutes. Then roll the edge back to expose the tape. Heat it and finish the seam. (You may be able to avoid this delay by running the iron up the wall on the first pass, but if the seam edges do not abut perfectly, the seam will be weak.) Groom the seam by cutting off any stray backing threads or loose ends of pile with a small scissors.

Stretching

First, decide which wall to stretch the carpet away from. Using a knee kicker, secure the carpet to the tackless strip on that side. Before you start adjust the tooth bite on a piece of scrap carpet. The teeth should just penetrate the backing when you activate the kicker.

To secure the first edge onto the tackless strip, bite the head of the kicker into the carpet about 1 inch from the wall. Lean on the arm handle and swiftly kick the cushion

Joining the Seam

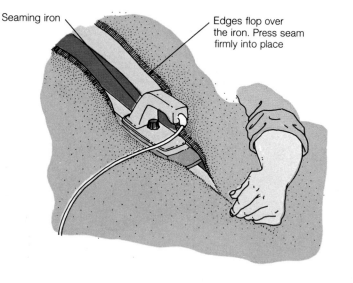

- Seaming iron
- Edges flop over the iron. Press seam firmly into place

with your knee. Proceed kick by kick, holding the secured carpet down on the strip with your hand so that it won't unhook. If the carpet is very stiff and won't fold tightly against the wall, force it a bit with a stair tool or a stretching paddle.

Follow the kicking and stretching sequence illustrated in the diagrams. For short distances (across hallways or small bedrooms, for example), use the knee kicker to stretch the carpet into place. Use a power stretcher for larger rooms. Adjust the teeth of the stretcher to the thickness of the carpet. Set the stretcher head 6 inches from the wall and adjust the extension tubes so that the foot presses against the opposite wall. Then press down on the lever to stretch the carpet toward the first wall. The lever should lock down into place with a gentle push. If the carpet does not move easily, lift the head and lower the handle a bit before biting into the carpet again. With the handle locked and the carpet stretched, fasten the section of carpet held by the stretcher head down onto the tackless strip. Use the side of a hammer or the trowellike paddle that comes with the stretcher to push the carpet down onto the pins. Then release the stretcher head, move it over 18 inches, and repeat the operation.

You or a partner will have to move the foot of the stretcher along the opposite wall as you proceed. Protect the baseboard or a weak wall with a piece of 2 by 4 long enough to span three or four studs. For added protection cover the 2 by 4 with a piece of scrap carpet. Set it between the foot of the stretcher and the wall.

Stretching Sequence

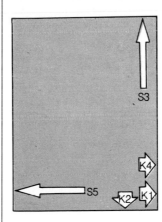

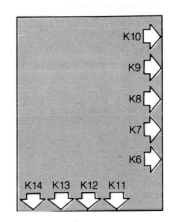

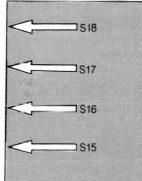

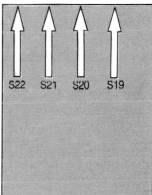

Stretching Carpet

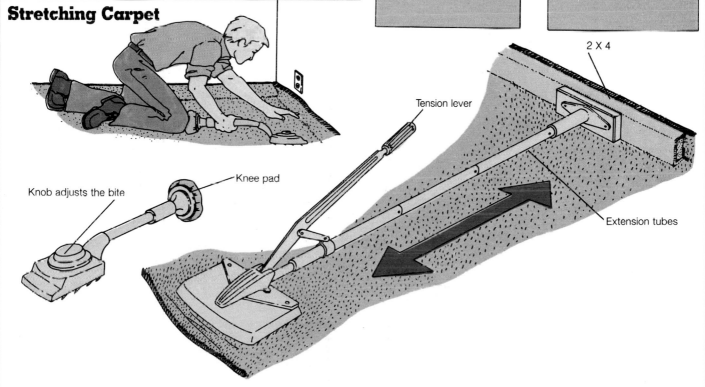

Knob adjusts the bite

Knee pad

Tension lever

2 X 4

Extension tubes

Trimming

Trim the carpet edges with a wall trimmer. Adjust it first to the thickness of the carpet. Start at the lapped end of the carpet, slicing downward at an angle until the trimmer is flat against the floor. Then hold the trimmer against both the wall and the floor and plow along the edge of the carpet. Carefully trim the last few inches with a utility knife. Tuck the trimmed carpet edge down into the gap between the tackless strip and the baseboard. Use a broad screwdriver or a stair tool, pushing it into the narrow section of carpet lapping over the gap, rather than down onto the very edge of the carpet itself. Otherwise the carpet will bulge and lift off the strip pins. Hit the screwdriver or stair tool with a rubber mallet to tuck stiff carpet down into the gap.

At doorways trim the edge of the carpet so that it centers under the closed door. If you installed a gripper edge on a concrete floor, flatten the metal flange over the carpet with a rubber mallet or a wood block and a hammer. If the edge of the carpet will be covered with a metal flat bar, nail it down first with tacks or 1-inch lath nails.

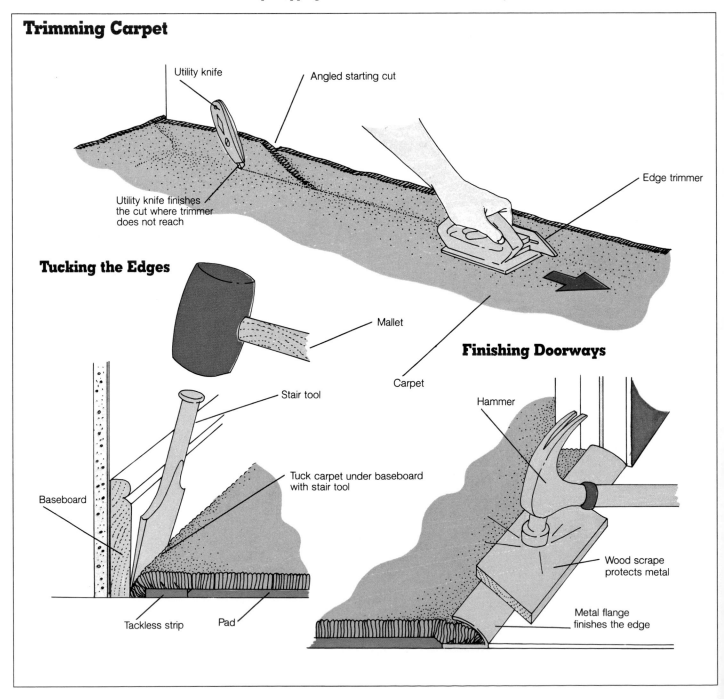

Trimming Carpet

Utility knife

Angled starting cut

Edge trimmer

Utility knife finishes the cut where trimmer does not reach

Tucking the Edges

Mallet

Carpet

Stair tool

Tuck carpet under baseboard with stair tool

Baseboard

Tackless strip

Pad

Finishing Doorways

Hammer

Wood scrape protects metal

Metal flange finishes the edge

INSTALLING CUSHION-BACKED CARPET

Cushion-backed carpet has its own bonded foam backing. It requires no stretching, since it is simply fixed to the existing floor with the appropriate adhesive. Although it is easier to install than conventional carpet, observe the same precautions. Poorly installed carpet will not wear well.

To Begin

The existing floor must be carefully prepared. Cushion-backed carpet is relatively thin, and irregularities in the subsurface will show through. If the subfloor has open knotholes or gouges, they should be filled and sanded smooth. Board subfloors or tongue-and-groove floors should be covered with an underlayment at least ¼ inch thick. Fill all the cracks and nail holes with floor filler.

Concrete subfloors must be completely free of moisture, since the foam backing of the carpet acts like a sponge. If the problem is minor, apply a coat of sealer to the subfloor. If moisture persists do not lay the carpeting. The use of cushion-backed carpet over plywood floors on sleepers or nailed directly to concrete is not recommended. Use conventional carpet instead.

Cushion-backed carpet can be laid directly on a tile floor if it is flat and dry, and if all the grout lines have been filled.

Don't remove the baseboards before installing cushion-backed carpet. The carpet edges will be tucked under them during trimming (see page 105).

Check all the doors to make sure that the carpet won't block their swing (see page 22). If it does, measure, mark, remove, and trim them.

Install a toothless binder bar with a flange that clamps down over the carpet to finish the edge at doorways. If the carpet must be seamed, follow the instructions in the next section. If not, rough-cut the carpet to size and then skip directly to the section on gluing it down.

The Carpet

Lay all the different pieces of carpet with the pile running in the same direction. Roll it out and rough-cut it, allowing a 3-inch margin at all floor perimeter edges. Cushion-backed carpet is always cut from the face side. Snap a chalk line on the floor where the seam will be placed. Carefully align one edge of the first piece of carpet

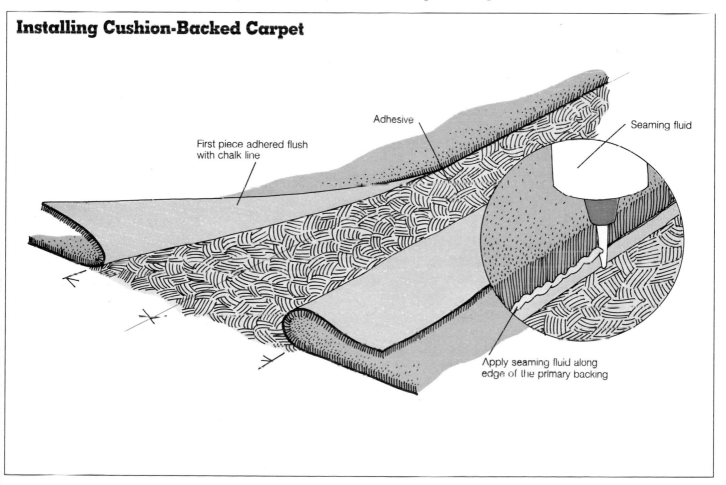

Installing Cushion-Backed Carpet

First piece adhered flush with chalk line

Adhesive

Seaming fluid

Apply seaming fluid along edge of the primary backing

with the chalk line. Place the second piece so that its edge overlaps the bottom piece by ¼ inch. Fold both edges back 2 or 3 feet and trowel a thin, even coat of adhesive onto the exposed floor. Carefully unfold the bottom piece, keeping the edge aligned exactly with the chalk line. Work the carpet with your hands to force air bubbles out to the edge.

Lay a bead of seaming fluid on the adhered piece of carpet along the edge of the primary backing material, avoiding getting any on the pile. Notch the applicator nozzle so that when you run its tip along the floor, the bead is expelled just at the height of the primary backing, not on the pile or foam.

Unfold the second piece of carpet back so that its edge tightly abuts the edge of the adhered piece. Be sure that the pattern, if any, lines up and that the pile of both pieces runs in the same direction. Since you allowed a ¼-inch overlap, the edges should press tightly together. The bulge produced by the ¼-inch allowance should be worked gently away from the seam. Where there are gaps, carefully rejoin both edges with your fingers until the entire seam is tight. Let the seam adhesive dry thoroughly before completing the installation. Snip off any loose ends of pile or backing threads.

Opposite: Rush mats and other nonpadded carpets should be installed over a subfloor prepared in the same manner as for cushion-backed carpets. Rush is a natural fiber that brings a striking textural quality to the rooms it is used in.

Gluing

Starting from the sidewalls, fold the untrimmed carpet edges in so that they don't bind against the wall. Then pull the whole piece back to the seam area, which is already adhered. If there is no seam, pull the single piece back until half the floor is exposed. Trowel adhesive onto the floor and roll the carpet over it toward the wall. Work out wrinkles or bumps with your hands as you go. Repeat the process for the other half of the carpet. If you have to deflate a bubble, poke it with an awl. Use a plastic syringe (available from carpet dealers) to inject contact adhesive into the hole. Press the carpet firmly onto the adhesive.

Trimming

Use a stair tool to seat and crease the edge of the carpet into the joint between the floor and the wall. Trim the carpet with a utility knife. Leave a margin equal to the thickness of the carpet and tuck it down against the wall with a stair tool. Flatten down any metal doorway flanges over the exposed edge of the carpet by placing a block of wood at one end and hitting it with a hammer, working your way across the flange. The wood will protect the flange from dents.

Note: Some carpet adhesives are noxious or even flammable. Read the manufacturer's instructions carefully, and make sure that the room is well ventilated. Extinguish nearby pilot lights and other open flames before using adhesives.

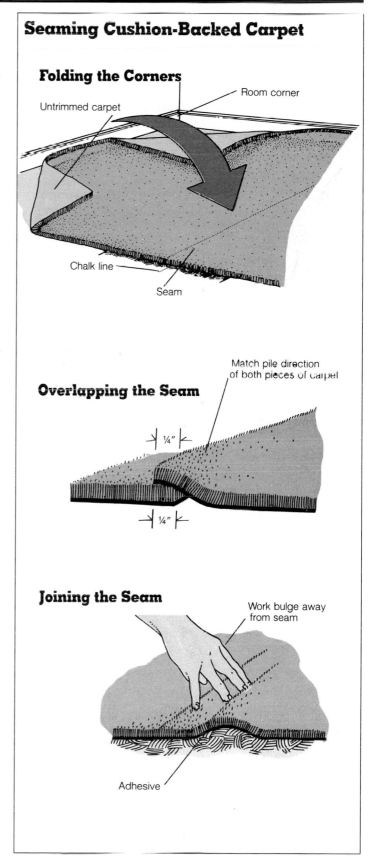

Seaming Cushion-Backed Carpet

Folding the Corners

Room corner

Untrimmed carpet

Chalk line

Seam

Overlapping the Seam

Match pile direction of both pieces of carpet

¼"

¼"

Joining the Seam

Work bulge away from seam

Adhesive

INSTALLING TRIM

Baseboards, thresholds, and other trim and finish details are important finishing touches of any new floor covering project. Visually, they integrate the floor with the walls. Functionally, they conceal and protect the perimeter gap. In selecting trim there are many options; the choice is generally a matter of personal preference.

To Begin

Before you install trim, take some time to properly store extra floor covering materials. If the installation project went well you should have approximately 5 percent of the materials remaining. Do not throw these away. Save extra wood, tiles, and pieces of resilient sheet and carpet for future repairs or remodeling projects. It is best to box extra flooring materials and to clearly label the boxes. Store these materials in a clean, dark, dry spot to prevent fading, molding, and animal damage. Plan to leave these boxes if you sell the house. New owners will appreciate having these materials on hand if a repair need arises.

Seal any extra paint, sealer, adhesive, and grout for use later. Clearly mark these containers with the floor covering they should be used on and the date last used. Dry products should last many years.

Properly dispose of any empty containers used for paint, sealer, adhesive, and grout. Do not simply toss these in your garbage can. Many of these products are toxic and should not end up in the ground fill of the local disposal site. Take the containers, rags, and other installation materials to a recycle center. If they can not dispose of them, check with the local sanitation department for proper disposal recommendations.

Protect the newly installed floor while finishing other construction around the house. Place plastic sheeting, carpet scraps, packing blankets, or sheets of plywood over just-laid floors. Be especially careful around edges before the baseboards, doors, and other trim is installed. These edges will not be protected and can be easily broken by foot falls and dropped tools. The exposed edges are also unprotected from moisture damage. Check that the edges have not become wet since installation. If there is moisture, dry out the edge with a hand-held dryer before installing baseboards.

Baseboards

Baseboard materials range from simple square-edge lumber to intricate wood moldings, vinyl cove base, and fancy ceramic border tiles. Buy wood or vinyl by the linear foot and cut it to fit as you go. Buy ceramic base border by the tile. There are a variety of trim pieces to cover the edges of carpet or resilient flooring where they abut adjacent floors.

Thresholds are available in hardwood (usually oak), metal, and real or synthetic stone. Wood and metal are easy to cut to length. Both are fastened to the subfloor with screws or nails. Buy stone thresholds cut to size. Glue them down with tile adhesives.

Wood Baseboards

Measure each length of board carefully; they should be cut to fit tight. Wherever two boards join along the wall, cut the ends at a 45-degree angle rather than square. This will prevent the joints from opening up as the material shrinks or the building moves. Make mitered joints at all outside corners. Inside corners should have butt joints for square-edge boards and special coped joints for molded boards. Attach the boards to the wall at each stud, using 6d or 8d finishing nails.

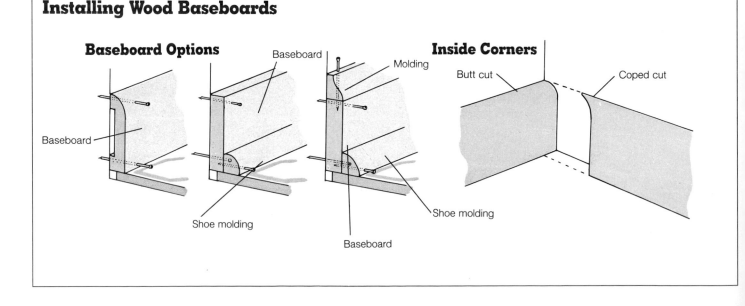

Installing Wood Baseboards

Baseboard Options — Baseboard · Baseboard · Molding · Baseboard · Shoe molding · Shoe molding · Baseboard

Inside Corners — Butt cut · Coped cut · Shoe molding

Installing Vinyl Cove Bases

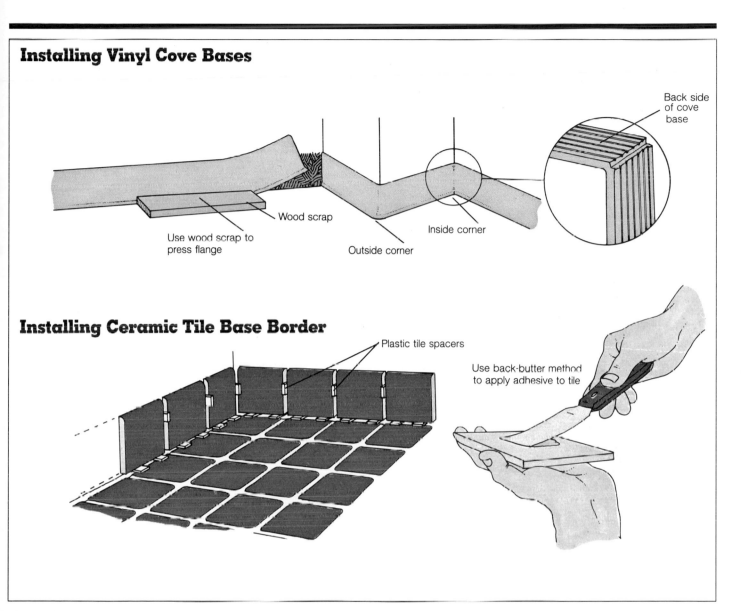

Back side of cove base

Use wood scrap to press flange

Wood scrap

Outside corner

Inside corner

Installing Ceramic Tile Base Border

Plastic tile spacers

Use back-butter method to apply adhesive to tile

Vinyl Cove Base

Vinyl cove base is attached to the wall with adhesive. Begin the installation in the corners and then fill in the straight lengths. Use a portable hair dryer to warm the vinyl before trying to bend it to fit corners. To fit an inside corner, cut a V notch in the base flange and lightly score the back from the notch to the top edge. To fit an outside corner, cut a V groove down the back, removing excess material from the groove. Don't notch the base flange, since it will stretch to wrap around the corner.

Some vinyl cove bases come with peel-and-stick backing. Others are attached with the same adhesive as that used for resilient flooring. Using a notched trowel or a putty knife, apply the adhesive to the wall as high as the base will cover. Press the base firmly into place. Wipe any adhesive from the wall with a rag.

Ceramic Border Tiles

For base borders use ceramic tile with one bullnose edge to provide a finished top. After the floor has been installed but prior to grouting, cut and fit each base border tile so that the grout lines on the floor continue into the border.

Start in one corner. Dry-fit the first tile and cut it to match the grout line on the floor. Then apply adhesive to the back of the tile, using the back-butter method (see page 86). Place plastic spacers at the floor and press the tile into place. As you set each successive tile in place, use both side spacers and floor spacers to keep the grout lines consistent. Grout the border and floor tiles at the same time following the directions on page 87.

Thresholds

Before installing a new wood threshold, undercut the door-stops if necessary. Then cut the threshold to length, predrill pilot holes, and attach it to the floor with 8d finishing nails.

Reducer Strips

To equalize floors of different heights, use a wood reducer strip instead of an ordinary threshold. The reducer is beveled so that its high edge is flush with the higher floor and its low edge is flush with the lower floor. This adjusts the level of the new flooring to that of the existing adjacent floor.

Installing Thresholds

Wood Thresholds

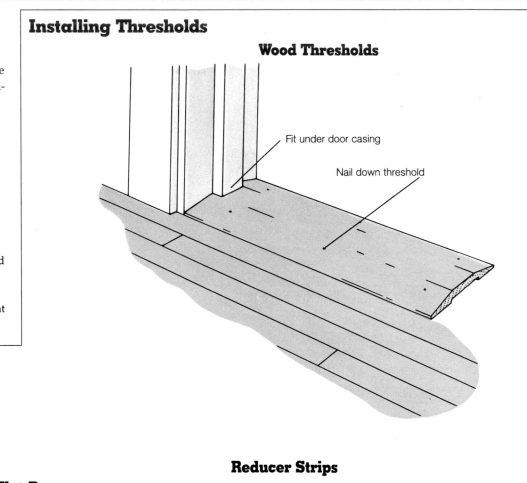

Fit under door casing

Nail down threshold

Reducer Strips

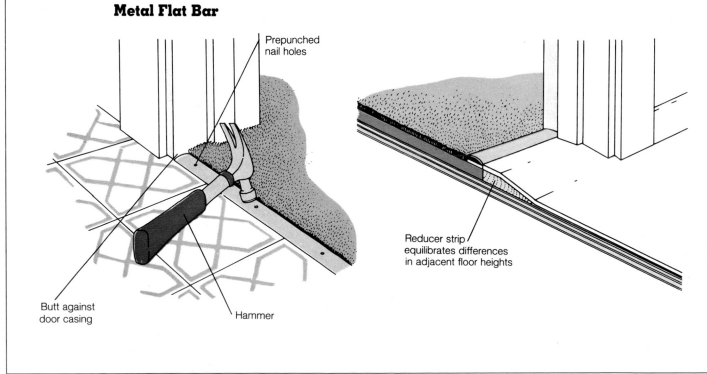

Metal Flat Bar

Prepunched nail holes

Butt against door casing

Hammer

Reducer strip equilibrates differences in adjacent floor heights

Finally! Your floor covering is installed, the trim is on, and the doors are rehung. Be sure to protect your new floor, such as this dimensioned stone tile, during the last stages of construction.

INDEX

111

U.S./Metric Measure Conversion Chart

		Formulas for Exact Measures			*Rounded Measures for Quick Reference*		
	Symbol	*When you know:*	*Multiply by:*	*To find:*			
Mass (Weight)	oz	ounces	28.35	grams	1 oz		= 30 g
	lb	pounds	0.45	kilograms	4 oz		= 115 g
	g	grams	0.035	ounces	8 oz		= 225 g
	kg	kilograms	2.2	pounds	16 oz	= 1 lb	= 450 g
					32 oz	= 2 lb	= 900 g
					36 oz	= 2¼ lb	= 1000 g (1 kg)
Volume	tsp	teaspoons	5.0	milliliters	¼ tsp	= 1/24 oz	= 1 ml
	tbsp	tablespoons	15.0	milliliters	½ tsp	= 1/12 oz	= 2 ml
	fl oz	fluid ounces	29.57	milliliters	1 tsp	= 1/6 oz	= 5 ml
	c	cups	0.24	liters	1 tbsp	= ½ oz	= 15 ml
	pt	pints	0.47	liters	1 c	= 8 oz	= 250 ml
	qt	quarts	0.95	liters	2 c (1 pt)	= 16 oz	= 500 ml
	gal	gallons	3.785	liters	4 c (1 qt)	= 32 oz	= 1 liter
	ml	milliliters	0.034	fluid ounces	4 qt (1 gal)	= 128 oz	= 3¾ liter
Length	in.	inches	2.54	centimeters	⅜ in.	= 1 cm	
	ft	feet	30.48	centimeters	1 in.	= 2.5 cm	
	yd	yards	0.9144	meters	2 in.	= 5 cm	
	mi	miles	1.609	kilometers	2½ in.	= 6.5 cm	
	km	kilometers	0.621	miles	12 in. (1 ft)	= 30 cm	
	m	meters	1.094	yards	1 yd	= 90 cm	
	cm	centimeters	0.39	inches	100 ft	= 30 m	
					1 mi	= 1.6 km	
Temperature	° F	Fahrenheit	5/9 (after subtracting 32)	Celsius	32° F	= 0° C	
					68°F	= 20°C	
	° C	Celsius	9/5 (then add 32)	Fahrenheit	212° F	= 100° C	
Area	in.²	square inches	6.452	square centimeters	1 in.²	= 6.5 cm²	
	ft²	square feet	929.0	square centimeters	1 ft²	= 930 cm²	
	yd²	square yards	8361.0	square centimeters	1 yd²	= 8360 cm²	
	a.	acres	0.4047	hectares	1 a.	= 4050 m²	